YESHIVATH BETH MOSHE
of Scranton, Pennsylvania is proud of its many
contributions to Torah scholarship. Since its
beginning in 1965, the Scranton Yeshiva has
elevated the calibre of Torah education through
its high school, beis medrash and Kollel-
Graduate Program.

Our alumni rank among the leading educators
and lay leaders in America.

Over the years, dissemination of valuable,
informative and spiritually uplifting Jewish
literature has become a tradition at Beth Moshe.
It is in this tradition that we present with pride
this current volume.

חובות הלבבות
שער הבטחון

Duties of the Heart
The Gate of Trust

Translated and Annotated by
Avraham Yaakov Finkel

YESHIVATH BETH MOSHE
SCRANTON, PA.

CONTENTS

הקדמה
מהראש ישיבה
מורינו הרב יעקב שניידמאן שליט"א

ספר חובת הלבבות נתקבל בכלל ישראל כפוסק אחרון בענ-
יני אמונת הי"ת ובחיובי עבודת ה'. ודבריו הועתקו כבר בספרי
הראשונים ואצ"ל בספרי האחרונים כמו השל"ה וכדומה. ובספר
מגיד מישרים להב"י כתוב דהמגיד צוה לו ללמוד בספר חובת
הלבבות בכל יום להכניע היצה"ר. וידוע עוד דהחתם סופר למד
עם תלמידיו בכל יום מספר חו"ה כמו עשר רגעים קודם שהתחיל
השיעור.

כל שער מהספר מבאר ענין אחד מאמונה ועבודה והשקפה.
וביאורו והסברתו הוא בדרך המיוחד לראשונים, שהם מקיפים
הסוגיא מכל צדיו ומבארים אותו בקיצור לשון עם ראיות מפסוקי
תנ"ך. ובכל שער יש כמה וכמה יסודות, ודבריו בנוין זה על זה,
וא"א לקלוט אותם בלימוד פעם אחת או שתים. ועיקר התועלת
הוא רק מחזרה כמה פעמים. ולא יאמר האדם דספר הזה קשה
ללמוד, דדבריו קצרים וענייניו עמוקים, דאדרבא קושי הספר מחייב
עיון רבה ולימוד לאט לאט, ועי"ז יצא תועלת הראוי.

שער הבטחון של חובת הלבבות הוא הספר הראשון המבאר
יסודות וחיובי בטחון בתורת מסכתא מיוחד על ענין הזה.

אמונת הי"ת נתחלק לשתי מדרגות. אחד חיוב אמונה הנוגע
רק ללב האדם, דהיינו שהוא מאמין בהי"ת ובאחדותו ואהבתו
ויראתו. שנית מדרגה של הנהגה למעשה, פירוש שמתוך אמונתו
נוהג בדרך מיוחד והוא הוא ההנהגה של הבוטח בהי"ת.

ובאמת

ובאמת הנהגת בטחון כבר מקובל בכלל ישראל בשיחתנו ובהנהגתנו, דהרי המשוחח עם חבירו וכן הכותב מכתב נהגו לומר אם ירצה הי"ת, או בלע"ז דאס איז בשערט. לשונות המורים על הבטחון בהי"ת ושהי"ת משגיח על כל מעשה. ולמרות כל זה בחרנו להדפיס שער הבטחון שלאחר העיון מראים הדברים דאדרבא חיוב הנהגת הבטחון צריך חיזוק ביותר. ויש ארבעה טעמים לזה.

טעם הראשון, הוא מה שכתב המסלת ישרים בהקדמתו וז"ל, כי לא תמצא ברוב דברי אלא דברים שרוב בנ"א יודעים אותם ולא מסתפקים בהם כלל, אלא שכפי רוב פרסומם וכנגד מה שאמיתתם גלויה לכל, כך ההעלם מהם מצוי מאד והשכחה רבה עכ"ל. ומבואר מדבריו דיש סכנה בענינים המפורסמים, דאינו מחשב ומעיין בו כראוי להבינו לעומקו, ויש לחוש שכל הביטויים שאנו משתמשים בהם נשארים משפה לחוץ. ורק בחזרה ומחשבה תמידית בשער הבטחון של חו"ה עד שהיא שגורה בפיו יכול לבא לידי הבנה אמיתית.

טעם שניה, מחמת גודל ההסתה מהיצר לנטות מדרך הבטחון הישרה, ואמרו חז"ל בפ"ק דברכות דף יב: תניא אחרי לבבכם זו מינות. ועיין רמב"ם פרק ב' מהל' עכו"ם הל' ג' דמבאר דדעתו של אדם קצרה ולא כל הדעות יכולים להשיג האמת על בוריו, ואם ימשך כל אדם אחר מחשבות לבו נמצא מחריב את העולם לפי קוצר דעתו וכו'. ומבואר ברמב"ם דלאו "ולא תתורו אחרי לבבכם" מחייב האדם להסיר מחשבות מינות וכדומה מלבו.

ולפי זה יתבונן האדם כמה קשה לאדם לנהוג בדרך בטחון הישרה. דהרי בכל מאורע חושב כמה מחשבות ולפי קוצר דעתו נופלים בלבו כמה ספקות. וכמעט א"א לפרוש ממחשבות המטים אותו מדרך הישרה. ואיך יכול להציל עצמו ממבוכה זה. והעצה היעוצה הוא לעיין ולחשוב בספר הזה, וממילא לא יחשוב המחשבות המטרידות אותו מדרך אמונה הראויה. ועיונו וחזרתו התמידית בספר הזה מעמיד האדם על הדרך הישר, ולבו ושכלו יהו מלאים מחשבות טהורות, וממילא יהא ניצל מיצה"ר זו של אחרי לבבכם.

טעם

טעם שלישית, שיש בענין בטחון סכנה עצומה משום דגם
באומות העולם נתקבל ענין של בטחון והשגחה. והנה בדבר שלא
נתקבל אצלם וכופרים בם אנו נזהרים לפרוש ממחשבותיהם, אבל
במה שגם הם מודים בו יש סכנה שאופן הבנתם בהנהגת בטחון
ישפיע עלינו. ולפי האמת דרכיהם רחוקים מאד מדרך התורה.

טעם רביעית (אשר נראה דהוא עולה על כל הטעמים) הוא
שבדורנו נתרבה הדפסת ספרים חיצונים עיתונים וגם יש "הרדיו"
וכדומה המודיעים לאדם כל מאורע שאירע, ובקשר לזה מבארים
למה אירע דבר פלוני, ולמה נפרצה מלחמה פלונית, ויש להם
חשבונות על גבי חשבונות לבאר כל דבר. וגם יש ספרים המבארים
איך להתעשר ואיך להנצל מעניות. ובאמת על כולם נאמר רבות
מחשבות בלב איש ועצת ה' היא תקום. ויש בדבריהם דברים
שמפתים לב האדם להאמינם, ובהשקפה ראשונה נראים דבריהם
מיוסדים על אדני היושר והשכל. ולדאבוננו כולנו שקועים ממש
במבול של דעות וחשבונות ומהלכים המתעים האדם מדרך
האמונה האמיתית. ורק ע"י לימוד ועיון בספר חו"ה יכולים אנו
לינצל מכל הדעות הכוזבות המסבבות אותנו.

בסולם בית אל לר' יעקב עמדין הובא מאמר נפלא וז"ל, ואיך
לא יבוש הכופר בהשגחה ונכלם מי שיעיין ביחוד עניננו ומעמדנו
בעולם, אנחנו האומה הגולה שה פזורה אחר כל מה שעבר עלינו
מהצרות והתמורות אלפים מהשנים ואין אומה בעולם נרדפת
כמונו, מה רבים היו צרינו, מה עצמו נשאו ראש הקמים עלינו
מנעורינו, להשמדינו לעקרנו לשרשנו מפני השנאה שסבתה הקנאה
רבת צררונו גם לא יכלו לנו לאבדנו ולכלותינו, כל האומות
הקדומות העצומות אבד זכרם בטל סברם, סר צלם, ואנו הדבקים
בה' כולנו חיים היום לא נפקד ממנו בכל תוקף אריכות גלותינו
אפילו אות וניקוד אחד מתורה שבכתב וכל דברי חכמים קיימים
לא יטה לארץ מנלם, לא שלט בהם יד הזמן ולא כלם, מה יענה
בזה פילוסוף חריף, היד מקרה עשתה כל אלה. חי נפשי כי
בהתבונני בנפלאות אלה, גדלו אצלי יותר מכל נסים ונפלאות
שעשה השי"ת לאבותנו במצרים ובמדבר ובארץ ישראל, וכל מה
שארך

שארך הגלות יותר נתאמת הנס יותר ונודע מעשה תקפו וגבורתו, בשגם כל הנביאים כבר ראו עומקו והתאוננו והתלוננו על אריכותו הנפלא בטרם היותו, והנה לא נפל מכל דבריהם ארצה, איה פה המכחיש וכו׳ ע״כ. וכדבריו כן הוא, דבדורותינו נתגדל הנס ביותר ובפרט שראינו יד ה׳ להתחיל קיבוץ גליות לא״י אשר ניבאו כל הנביאים דכן יהיה באחרית הימים.

ומ״מ יש פיתויי היצר לחשוב חשבונות אנושיית בקיום כלל ישראל ולומר דהצלתנו תלוי בהשתדלות אנושיית. ולא חושבים דאם קיומינו והצלתנו הוא נס נגלה א״כ מוטל עלינו לעיין מהו רצון הי״ת, דהרי הוא המשגיח עלינו והמדריך אותנו, ואך ורק זה תקוותנו.

וכמו כן אישי הפרטי אילו יעיין כראוי בחייו ובכל שאירע לו יראה דיד ה׳ עשתה כל זאת ולא יפתה עצמו דהשתדלותו עשתה את החיל הזה.

והי״ת יסייע את עמו להיות בוטחים בו ונזכה עי״ז לראות ישועת הקב״ה וצמיחת הגאולה.

TRANSLATION OF
RABBI YAAKOV SCHNAIDMAN'S
PROLOGUE

Chovos Halevavos—Duties of the Heart—is universally recognized as the most comprehensive and authoritative work on the subject of faith in Hashem and the obligation of serving Him this entails. This work is widely quoted by early and later authorities including the *Sheloh* (Rabbi Yeshaya Horowitz 1560-1630) and the *Beis Yosef* (Rabbi Yosef Caro, author of the Shulchan Aruch 1488-1575). The latter relates in his *Maggid Meisharim* that the *maggid*, a heavenly spirit, urged him to study Duties of the Heart every day as means of mastering his *yetzer hara*—evil inclination. It is a well-known fact that the Chasam Sofer (Rabbi Moshe Sofer of Pressburg 1763-1839) lectured on *Duties of the Heart* for fifteen minutes every day before beginning his Gemara discourse.

Each section of *Duties of the Heart* deals with a subject relating to faith, prayer and fundamental beliefs. The author's approach is to analyze the topic at hand briefly and concisely and to corroborate his conclusions by citing Biblical verses. Each chapter deals with a number of important doctrines which should be studied in depth. Skimming over the pages is of little value; the greatest benefit from this work can be gained only after probing its teachings

---

Rabbi Yaakov Schnaidman is the Rosh Yeshivah of Yeshivath Beth Moshe Scranton, Pennsylvania.

time and again. Don't say that the literary style of *Duties of the Heart* and its profound subject matter make it too difficult to grasp. Consider it a challenge, and if you put your mind to it and study it at a slow pace, you will achieve the hoped for result.

The section called *Shaar Habitachon*—The Gate of Trust—which has been translated into English in the present volume—is the first work ever written that offers a systematic exposition of the principles and obligations of trusting in Hashem. We learn that trusting in Hashem must be done on two levels: On a spiritual level, so that we should believe intellectually and rationally in the existence and Oneness of Hashem, love Him and be in awe of Him. And on a practical level, in that we should conduct ourselves in a way that reflects our trust in Hashem.

Bitachon—trust and faith in Hashem—is a concept that is familiar to every Jew. It is ingrained in the Jewish personality to the point that it has become part of our every-day vocabulary. When we talk or write about plans for the future, we invariable use the expression "*Im yirtzeh Hashem*—God willing." Whatever happens to us, our first reaction is to say, "It was *bashert*—It was Hashem's will." The thought we are conveying thereby is, that we have faith and firmly believe that Hashem guides our destiny and the fate of the world.

Now the question may be raised, since *bitachon* seems to be an integral part of our thought processes, why, of all the themes in *Duties of the Heart* did we choose The Gate of Trust for the present translation? On reflection we can think of four reasons why the concept of *bitachon*, more than any other idea, needs to be strengthened and reinforced.

First, as Rabbi Moshe Chaim Luzzatto says in his introduction to *Mesillas Yesharim*, "It is my aim to direct the reader's attention to certain well known and generally accepted truths. For the very fact that they are well known and generally accepted is the cause that they are being overlooked." What he means to say is that there is a danger that you do not investigate and analyze things you take as self-evident truths, and phrases we use to express our faith are just platitudes and tired cliches. With that in mind you realize that you can gain a true understanding of The Gate or Trust only by constantly reviewing its chapters until you commit them to memory.

Second, the study of *bitachon* is important because the evil inclination is trying without letup to weaken our faith in Hashem. In fact, the Gemara in Berachos (12b) interprets the passage, *"So that you do not follow your heart" (Bamidbar 15:39)* to mean "so that you do not fall victim to heresy". The Rambam (*Hilchos Akum 2:3*) explains that most people are not mentally equipped to comprehend the absolute truth, and if every person would follow the dictates of his own limited reasoning power, the world would come to an end. Therefore, says the Rambam, the commandment of "do not follow your heart" demands that we banish any thoughts that tend to undermine our faith. If you think about it, you realize how difficult it is to maintain perfect faith. Any event that occurs in the world stirs a number of conflicting thoughts in our minds, and it is almost inevitable that certain doubts arise. At times like this, how is a person to extricate himself from inner confusion and settle his doubts? The answer can be found in the pages of The Gate of Trust. It will dispel any thoughts of skepticism and misgivings, and will bring the wavering heart back to the right path. It will fill the mind with pure thinking, and thereby the seductive schemes of the evil inclination will be foiled.

Third, the subject of faith holds within it a grave peril, because the notions of faith and Divine providence are accepted also in non-Jewish theology. When it comes to religious doctrines that are in conflict with our beliefs it is clear to us that we may not give them any credence, but in matters where they seem to agree with our beliefs, such as the principles of trust there is the danger that the non-Jewish interpretation will influence our thinking. It should be noted that the non-Jewish perspective on faith and trust varies greatly from the Torah view on *bitachon*.

Fourth, and most important, in our day and age, there is a proliferation of secular literature, books and publications. The press and the media instantly publish and transmit any event, and offer "learned" commentaries on the whys and wherefores of global developments. Analysts present background information on every political, economic or military situation that arises. There is a plethora of books that offer advice on how to succeed in business or any other field of endeavor. But we know the truth, that *"Many designs are in a man's mind, but the plan of Hashem—only it—is accomplished" (Mishlei 19:21)*. At first glance, the news analyses and editorials seem to make sense, and we easily forget that we are drowning in a morass of opinions and conjectures that are designed to lure us away from the road of true faith. It is only by in-depth study of *Duties of the Heart* and The Gate of Trust in particular, that we can become immune to the false doctrines and ideologies that threaten to engulf us.

Rabbi Yaakov Emden (1698-1776), in a fascinating discourse in *Sulam Beis El* states, "How can a non-believer not be embarrassed and humiliated when he reflects on the uniqueness of the Jewish people in the world. Here we are, a nation in exile, a lost sheep among the nations. After two thousand years of oppression and tyranny there is not a nation in the world that has been persecuted like us. Countless tormentors, driven by insane hatred, attempted to wipe us out. No matter how hard they tried, they could not overcome us. All the mighty nations of antiquity have disappeared, their memory has faded into oblivion. But we who cling to Hashem are still here! We survived all the horrors of the long exile. Our Torah has survived intact; not one letter, vowel or punctuation mark of the written Torah is missing. All the words of the Sages of the Oral Torah have been preserved. The ravages of time have not eroded it. What explanation can you, brilliant philosopher, offer for this? Did it just happen by accident, by mere chance? By my life, when I contemplate these miracles of our survival in exile, I find that they are far greater than all the miracles that *Hashem Yisbarach* performed for our ancestors in Egypt, in the wilderness and in Eretz Yisrael. The longer we are in exile the more the miracle of our survival becomes evident, and His mighty deeds become apparent. Indeed, all the prophets saw visions of the terror of the exile and sorrowfully raised their voices against its long duration long before it came to pass. And everything transpired exactly like they predicted it. Can anyone deny it?"

Rabbi Yaakov Emden's words are undeniably true. Hashem's

miracles have become even more evident in the recent past as we are witnessing Hashem's hand in the ingathering of the exiles from the four corners of the earth to Eretz Yisrael, in fulfillment of the prophetic predictions of the end of days.

In spite of these clear manifestations of Hashem's guidance, the evil inclination tries to entice us into thinking that our problems can be solved through human efforts and political stratagems. We do not realize that if our survival is an overt Divine miracle, then we have to discern what it is that Hashem wants us to do. After all, He is the One who watches over us and guides our destiny; and doing His will is our only hope.

On an individual level, if a person scrutinizes his life and recognizes Hashem's close supervision in everything that is happening to him, he will not fall prey to the evil inclination's insistence that he himself is the master of his fate.

May Hashem help us to attain faith and trust in Him, so that we will deserve His salvation and the sprouting of our redemption.

TRANSLATOR'S INTRODUCTION

WHAT ARE THE DUTIES OF THE HEART?

―――――◦◉◦―――――

Chovos Halevavos—Duties of the Heart—written by Rabbeinu Bachya ibn Pakudah has been described as perhaps the most noble work of post-Talmudic literature on the subject of Torah ethics. Its influence on Jewish history has been immense. For close to a thousand years it has uplifted and revitalized Jewry and lent a new dimension to all of the time-honored aspects of Jewish life.

In the ten sections of *Duties of the Heart* the author shows us that side by side with the emphasis on performance of *mitzvos*, such as *tzitzis, tefillin, matzah* and *sukkah*, which he characterizes as the "duties of the limbs" the Torah stresses the importance of cultivating the proper spirit and frame of mind, which he calls the "duties of the heart". They include both positive and negative commandments. Positive commandments include believing in Hashem, accepting His Oneness, fearing Him, loving Him, trusting Him, and loving your neighbor. Negative commandments include not hating your brother, not being envious, not bearing a grudge, and not taking revenge.

Thus every *mitzvah* must be performed jointly by the body and the heart: our limbs doing the physical act of the *mitzvah*, and our heart providing the proper *kavanah*—intent. In fact, the "duties of the heart" form the very foundation of all the *mitzvos*, and without the appropriate intentions, it would be impossible for us to keep any of the physical *mitzvos*.

Rabbeinu Bachya noted that, although the concept of "duties of the heart" was dealt with in various passages in the Torah, the Prophets and the Talmud, it was not set down in an organized, systematic pattern. Recognizing the need for a methodical, rational and yet traditional explanation of the "duties of the heart" he set out, after much hesitation, to fill the need. He meant *Duties of the Heart* to be a practical and edifying guide. His purpose was to educate and encourage people to lead a life based on piety, Torah ethics and character refinement.

In the same spirit in which the Sages of the Talmud cited scriptural support for every thought they propounded, Rabbeinu Bachya ibn Pakuda shows how each of the principles in *Duties of the Heart*, besides being grounded in logic and reason, is based on a multitude of passages from the Torah, the prophets, and the teachings of the Sages in the Talmud. For example, he demonstrates the overriding importance of doing a *mitzvah* with the proper intent by showing that the Torah greatly differentiates between an act that was done intentionally and one done unwittingly. He points out that in the case of murder, there is a vast difference between premeditated murder and accidental manslaughter; the intentional murderer receives the death penalty, whereas a person guilty of accidental homicide is sentenced to exile in one of the cities of refuge. Intent makes all the difference. So too, when it comes to the performance of *mitzvos*, intent and *kavanah* are indispensable requirements.

In the ten sections—Gates—of *Duties of the Heart*, the author defines the basic principles of the Jewish faith. He explains that they are not stated specifically in the Torah, because the Torah trusted that we would derive them by ourselves. Therefore, he urges us thoughout his book to examine, scrutinize and explore the duties of the heart rather than accept them at face value. Then, if we perform the *mitzvos* in conjunction with "the duties of the heart", we will attain greater attachment to Hashem and merit to perceive the celestial Light.

THE TEN GATES

1. *Shaar Hayichud*—The Gate of Wholehearted Belief in Hashem's Oneness.
2. *Shaar Habechinah*—The Gate of Recognition of Hashem's Wisdom, Power and Goodness.
3. *Shaar Avodas Elokim*—The Gate of the Duty to Serve Hashem.
4. *Shaar Habitachon*—The Gate of Trust.
5. *Shaar Yichud Hamaaseh*—The Gate of Dedication of Purpose.
6. *Shaar Hakeniah*—The Gate of Humility.
7. *Shaar Hateshuvah*—The Gate of Repentance.
8. *Shaar Cheshbon Hanefesh*—The Gate of Self-Examination
9. *Shaar Haperishus*—The Gate of Self-Denial.
10. *Shaar Ahavas Hashem*—The Gate to Loving Hashem.

A BRIEF SYNOPSIS OF THE TEN GATES

The First Gate, *Shaar Hayichud*—The Gate of Unity—elaborates on the author's contention that belief in the existence and unity of Hashem should rest not solely on faith, but should be bolstered by conviction based on rationalistic investigation. In a profound analysis Rabbeinu Bachya ibn Pakudah establishes that there is a Creator Who created the world out of nothing. With brilliant arguments he refutes the false theory of the non-believers who say that the universe came into being by itself. "I cannot imagine any sane person saying such a thing!" he exclaims. He explains that if you would see an irrigation wheel that waters a field, would anyone say that it had appeared out of the blue, without a skilled craftsman who designed and made it? Another illustration: If someone showed you a piece of writing and tried to convince you that he splattered ink which formed itself into that written piece, wouldn't you call him a liar to his face? How then could anyone possibly believe that the universe which is infinitely more mysterious and complex came about by chance, without the wisdom of Hashem behind it? Are not the celestial wheels of the galaxies, and the orbits of the planets greater marvels than an irrigation wheel?

The Second Gate, *Shaar Habechinah*—The Gate of Recognition—deals with our obligation to recognize the kindness Hashem bestows on us, and to acknowledge His wisdom, His power and His goodness as they are evident in the universe.

The Third Gate, *Shaar Avodas Elokim*—The Gate of Service to Hashem—tells us how we should respond to Hashem's kindness and show our gratitude to Him. It explains how with the help of Torah study and the performance of *mitzvos* we can overcome the temptations of the evil inclination. We learn under what circumstances we should use either one of the opposing character traits such as fear and hope, shame and impudence, anger and goodwill, compassion and callousness, pride and humility, love and hate, generosity and miserliness, laziness and diligence.

The Fourth Gate, *Shaar Habitachon*—The Gate of Trust—the subject of this translation, will be discussed in greater detail below.

The Fifth Gate, *Shaar Yichud Hamaaseh*—The Gate of Dedication of Purpose—gives you a clearer insight in the ploys of the evil inclination and the inducements it uses to defeat you and to encourage you to indulge in worldly pleasures. When the evil inclination loses hope of making you accept that, it makes you doubt the existence of Hashem. If that fails, it tries to make you doubt the truth of the Torah, the Oral Torah and the doctrine of reward and punishment. When all these tactics fail, it will make you lazy in your service to Hashem and make you focus on worldly things like food, drink, dress, and satisfying your bodily desires. But if you are aware of the evil inclination's tricks, you will be vigilant, and Hashem will rescue you from its snare.

The Sixth Gate, *Shaar Hakeniah*—The Gate of Humility—discusses the ways we can attain humility. If we realize Hashem's exaltedness, greatness and incomparability, and that "every being's destiny is dust" and that "sand and a clump of earth will be your dwelling place", then we cannot help but become meek and humble. We learn that being humble means: acting kindly, judging others favorably, always forgiving, doing everything in a spirit of surrender, belittling our achievements, asking Hashem for help, speaking little and in a low voice, making few jokes, refraining from haughtiness, never insulting, and not indulging in worldly pleasures. Above all, to avoid arrogance.

The Seventh Gate, *Shaar Hateshuvah*—The Gate to Repentance—stresses the saying of our Sages that "the gates of repentance are never closed to you, and nothing will ever deter you if you really want to draw closer to Hashem." Rabbi Bachya ibn Pakudah exhorts us, "Wake up, hurry, and have pity on your soul! And shame on you for acting to Hashem in ways you would not even act toward a human being!" He warns us, "Spare yourself for the inevitable, which is fast approaching. And do not think it is too late to repent. It is not!"

The Eighth Gate, *Shaar Cheshbon Hanefesh*—The Gate of Self-Examination—tells you to meditate on "what you have done already, as well as what you have to do from now on." You should look at your inner self as an outside observer and gauge how well you are doing. As a guide toward self-assessment the Eighth Gate lists thirty things that you should realize intensely, including, that Hashem created you as an act of kindness, that He gave you a body and an intellect, that He gave you the Torah, that you should serve Him diligently and ceaselessly, and that you should work with others to better the world. The noble effects of introspection are that you acquire good traits, your doubts are resolved, your mind becomes enlightened, your evil inclination withdraws, you comprehend great things and you are able to unravel mysteries.

The Ninth Gate, *Shaar Haperishus*—The Gate of Self-Denial defines a person who abstains as one who has the opportunity to act on his desires and does not. The proper kind of abstinence for a Torah-observant Jew is to do away with all excesses, because then reason dominates desire. There are three forms of abstinence: extreme, moderate and lenient. Those who are lenient in their abstinence separate themselves from the world in their hearts but join in the development of society. This form of abstinence is most in line with the Torah.

The Tenth Gate, *Shaar Ahavas Hashem*—The Gate to Loving Hashem—calls the love of Hashem "the greatest quality to have and the highest level of service to Hashem humanly possible. . . Every *mitzvah* and good character trait is a step toward the love of Hashem, which is their aim and their purpose." The question is raised: Since Hashem is "an All-consuming Fire" how is it humanly possible to love Hashem and draw close to Him? We are shown a number of ways in which we can demonstrate our love of Hashem, such as guiding and instructing others in how to serve Hashem, as it says, *"All those who teach righteousness to the multitudes will shine like the stars for ever and ever" (Daniel 12:3)*, and by not praying without first feeling it in your heart, for a short prayer said devoutly is better than a longer one said quickly and without heart.

Rabbeinu Bachya ibn Pakudah urges you to "delve into this book and read it, memorize its contents, observe its priciples, and ponder your progress at all times. . . You will be set straight by this book and will set others straight by it."

The Gate of Trust

The Fourth Gate, *Shaar Habitachon*—The Gate of Trust—has been chosen as the subject of the present translation. The Gate of Trust is unique in its pioneering spirit, for it is the first work in Torah literature to explain in an organized, logical and definitive manner the fundamental principles of *bitachon*—faith in Hashem. It tells us the great benefits to trusting Hashem, such as, freedom from worldly cares, peace of mind, security and tranquility. Its premise is that a person who has *bitachon* trusts that Hashem will do only what is best for him.

In that connection The Gate of Trust raises the often-heard

question: If you trust in Hashem, why is it necessary for you to work in order to earn a livelihood? Why doesn't Hashem provide your needs without you having to labor? The reason given is that Hashem tests you with worldly needs to see if you serve Him or rebel against Him. Also, if a person did not have to earn a livelihood, in his affluence he would not feel dependent on Hashem and would turn his back on Him; in his life of abundance and leisure he would surely go astray and become corrupt, as it says, *"Jeshurun became fat, and it kicked" (Devarim 32:15)*. The Mishnah expresses this idea in the saying, "Torah study is good together with an occupation" (Avos 2:2).

The Gate of Trust asks the age-old question: Why is it that sometimes we see righteous people having to work hard for a living, while many sinners are able to enjoy a good and easy life? We are told that one of the reasons the righteous suffer is that they may have committed a sin that they must pay for here, in this world, so that they will enjoy undiminished bliss in the World to Come. Then again, they suffer to show their patience, and to be an example to others, like in the case of Iyov. Sometimes Hashem afflicts the righteous with poverty and illness in order for them to demonstrate their piety and continued service to Hashem in spite of their troubles. And why is Hashem kind to the wicked? Because of something good they may have done in the past for which they are rewarded in this world. It may also be that the wicked person's good fortune may actually be his undoing or even kill him, or possibly it may come to him because of a good deed his father did in the past.

Have faith in Hashem in matters of health and sickness, says *Duties of the Heart*, but always try to stay healthy and avoid sickness in the usual ways. Trust Hashem, and He will heal you of your illnesses whether you use remedies or not.

One of the topics The Gate of Trust focuses on, is a problem that has baffled thinkers of every generation: Why does the Torah tell us nothing explicitly about reward and punishment in the World to Come, and speaks of it only in veiled allusion? Several answers are given: First, we know nothing about the state of the soul without a body, much less about what gives the soul delight or troubles it. Also, since historically the idea of reward and punishment in the World to Come was transmitted to the people by the prophets and sages of every generation, the prophets saw no need to write it down. Furthermore, Hashem promised His people an immediate reward or punishment in this world, for He knew that as soon as they would be ready to serve Him, they would understand by their own reasoning the spiritual nature of the reward and punishment that are in store for them in the World to Come. Thus it did not need to be written down in the Torah and the books of the Prophets. Another reason is that the essence of reward in the World to Come is attachment to Hashem and the coming closer to His heavenly Light, which are concepts that cannot be expressed in human terms.

The Gate of Trust reinforces our trust in Hashem and teaches us to accept His judgment, as Rabbeinu Bachya puts it, "The more you know about Hashem, and the more you believe that He guides you and provides for you, the more you will trust Him."

RABBEINU BACHYA BEN YOSEF IBN PAKUDAH

Very little is known about the illustrious author of *Duties of the Heart*. The only data we have is that he lived in the second half of the 11th century, and that he was a *dayan*—judge of a rabbinical court—in the city of Saragossa in Moslem Spain. The era was the Golden Age of Spanish Jewry, when Rabbi Shmuel Hanagid, a great Talmud scholar, was an influential statesman in the province of Granada. Rabbeinu Bachya was a contemporay of Rabbi Shlomo ibn Gabirol, the famous grammarian and poet who wrote *Tikkun Middos Hanefesh*. He probably knew the *Rif* (Rabbi Yitzchak Alfasi) who came to Spain in 1088, and was appointed Rabbi of Lucena. It was a time when Torah flourished in Spain. Best known are two towering Torah personalities who lived during that era: Rabbi Yehudah Halevi (1080-1145), the celebrated philosopher and poet who wrote the *Kuzari*, and Rabbi Avraham Ibn Ezra

(1089-1164), the great commentator of Tanach. Rabbeinu Bachya was greatly influenced and often refers to the writings of Rabbeinu Saadyah Gaon (892-942) who wrote *Emunos Vedeyos*, the first work of philosophic speculation and proof.

THE *SEFER CHOVOS HALEVAVOS*— DUTIES OF THE HEART

Duties of the Heart was written and published in 1080. It was written in Arabic, under the title of *al-Hidayah ila fara' id al qulub*, "Guidance to the Duties of the Heart".

Rabbeinu Bachya wrote this book both for Torah scholars and beginners, and for those who have strayed and are looking for guidance to return to Hashem and the Torah. In Rabbeinu Bachya's time the vast majority of the Jewish people lived in North Africa, Egypt, Spain, Eretz Yisrael and Persia, under Moslem domination. They spoke Arabic, and many Rabbis wrote their works in that language. It was for this reason that he wrote it in Arabic, as he puts it, "in order that the things I want to explain should be easy to understand." Less than one hundred years after its publication, the book had gained universal acclaim and was studied widely in the Arabic original. But as the Jewish population moved into France and Italy where no Arabic was spoken, a Hebrew translation was needed. The first such translation was produced by Rabbi Yehudah ibn Tibbon, in 1161. He translated many other works, including *Emunos Vedeyos*, and the *Kuzari*. In his translation of *Duties of the Heart* he faithfully adheres to the Arabic original, giving a literal rendition of the nuances and idiomatic expressions of the text which in many instances makes the text obscure and incomprehensible. A second translation was done by Rabbi Yosef Kimchi in which he paraphrased difficult phrases. However, only one section of this translation has survived, so that Rabbi Yehudah ibn Tibbon's work is the only version available.

TRANSLATIONS AND COMMENTARIES

Duties of the Heart was first printed in Naples in 1490, and again in Bologna in 1548. Many commentaries on the work have been written, including two classic works: *Marpe Lanefesh* by Rabbi Refael ben R. Zechariah Mandel of Frankfurt a.m. (Frankfurt a.M., 1867) and *Pas Lechem* by Rabbi Chaim Avraham ben Rabbi Aryeh Leib Katz of Mohilev, (Shklov, 1803). I used both these commentaries extensively in my translation. More recently, a translation from the Arabic into Hebrew was done by Rabbi Yosef Kapach who used, among others, an ancient and very accurate Yemenite manuscript (Jerusalem, 1973). In 1968, a new translation appeared in Jerusalem entitled Lev Tov, by Rabbi Pinchas Yehudah Lieberman who rendered the Ibn Tibbon text into contemporary modern Hebrew.

Over the centuries *Duties of the Heart* has proved to be a timeless classic. Great Torah luminaries like Rabbi Yosef Karo, (the author of the Shulchan Aruch) and Rabbi Yitzchak Luria (the holy Arizal), studied it daily. The Vilna Gaon, Rabbi Pinchas of Koretz, and Rabbi Elimelech of Lizhensk (the No'am Elimelech) immersed themselves in the *sefer* and encouraged others to do likewise. The Chasam Sofer was called "a living Duties of the Heart". The revival of Torah that has taken place through the movements of *Mussar* and *Chasidus* was sparked by *Duties of the Heart*. Rabbi Yisrael Salanter, the founder of the *Mussar* movement made it the primer of the movement. Today *Duties of the Heart* is avidly studied in many yeshivahs and chasidic study halls. It has been reprinted numerous times and can be found on the shelves of every yeshivah, *beis midrash*, and most public and private home libraries.

In this translation I have tried to present the text of The Gate of Trust as faithfully as possible, in informal, conversational English. Occasionally the difficult syntax made it necessary to paraphrase passages that otherwise would have been totally obscure. I hope that the study of The Gate of Trust will stimulate the reader to study *Duties of the Heart* in its entirety, *lehagdil Torah ulehadirah*.

AVRAHAM YAAKOV FINKEL
KISLEV, 5758/1997

DUTIES OF THE HEART
GATE FOUR

The Gate of Trust in God
On Trusting God Alone

INTRODUCTION

———◉———

After having discussed our duty to serve God, I decided to continue by focusing on the quality one who serves God needs most. That quality is to trust God in all phases of life, for trust in God is very helpful for one's Torah observance and worldly affairs.

Trusting in God will help your Torah observance by giving you serenity and peace of mind. A person must trust God like a servant trusts his master. He who does not place his trust in God is by definition trusting someone or something other than God. God then removes His Divine supervision from him and leaves him in the care of the one he trusts. He will become like those described in the following verses, *"For My people have committed two evils: They have forsaken Me, the Source of living waters, to dig for themselves cisterns, broken cisterns that cannot even hold water"* (Yirmeyah 2:13), and *"They exchanged their Glory for the image of a bull that feeds on grass"* (Tehillim 106:20). It also says, *"Blessed is the man who trusts in Hashem, then Hashem will be his security"* (Yirmeyah 17:7). *"Praiseworthy is the man who has made Hashem his trust, and did not turn to the arrogant and to followers of falsehood"* (Tehillim 40:5), and *"Cursed is the man who trusts in people and makes flesh [and blood] his strength and turns his heart away from Hashem"* (Yirmeyah 17:5).

If a person relies on his wisdom, skill, physical strength or efforts, he will waste his energy, become exhausted, and ultimately his ingenuity will fall short of achieving his purpose. As it says, *"He traps the shrewd with their trickery"* (Iyov 5:13), and *"Once more I saw under the sun that the race is not won by the swift, nor the battle by the strong"* (Koheles 9:11), and *"Young lions may want and hunger, but those who seek Hashem will not lack any good"* (Tehillim 34:11).

If a person relies on his wealth, either it will be taken from him, and he will wind up penniless, or, he will not be able to enjoy his wealth. As it says, *"He lies down, a rich man, [his wealth] intact; when he opens his eyes it is gone"* (Iyov 27:19), and furthermore it says, *"Do not work hard to gain wealth. Have the sense to desist. . . You see it, then it is gone"* (Mishlei 23:4,5), and *"In the middle of his days [his wealth] will leave him"* (Yirmeyah 17:11). The wise [Shlomoh Hamelech] said, *"God sometimes grants a man riches, property and wealth . . . yet God does not permit him to enjoy it"* (Koheles 6:2). His wealth is merely on deposit with him, to guard against loss, until it will land up in the hands of the person for whom it was intended, as it says, *"To the sinner He has given the urge to gather and amass—that he may give it over to one who is pleasing to God"* (Koheles 2:26), and *"[The wicked man] may prepare [a wardrobe], but a righteous man will wear it, and the virtuous man will divide the money"* (Iyov 27:17).

Wealth may cause a person's downfall and bring about the loss of his soul. For it says, *"There is a grave evil which I have seen under the sun; riches hoarded by their owner to his misfortune"* (Koheles 5:12).

TRUST IN GOD MAKES YOU INDEPENDENT

Another advantage of trusting in God is that you will not come to serve anyone other than God. You will not place your hope in anyone nor will you depend on anyone. You will not cater to people in order to get into their good graces, nor will you flatter them. You won't agree to associate with them when they intend to transgress the service of God. You will not be intimidated by their actions, and you will not be afraid to argue against them. Rather, you will be free [to express your opinion in the service of God] because you are not dependent on their favors, and thus not compelled to thank and repay them. If you have to criticize them, you will not be afraid to hurt their feelings. If it is necessary for you to humiliate them [for their evil ways], you will not be bashful. You will not have to validate their crooked deeds, as the prophet puts it, *"For Hashem, God helps me, therefore I was not humiliated; therefore I made my face as hard as flint and knew that I would not be ashamed" (Yeshayah 50:7)*, and *"Don't be afraid of them, and don't be afraid of their words... Don't fear their words, and don't be intimidated by them" (Yechezkel 2:6); "Do not be afraid of them" (Yirmeyah 1:8)*, and *"Don't be frightened of them" (ibid. v. 17)*; and *"I have made your forehead like a metal stronger than flint; do not fear them, and do not be intimidated before them" (Yechezkel 3:9)*.

PEACE OF MIND AND SERENITY

Another benefit of trusting in God is that one who relies on God will be able to detach himself from worldly concerns [like worrying about his livelihood] and devote himself entirely to serving God.

> The alchemist could supposedly change base metals into precious ones. One who trusts in God has less worries than the alchemist who was considered the epitome of the worry free, because his livelihood was always readily available.

He will have inner tranquility, peace of mind, and complacency about worldly matters as does the alchemist—a person who has the knowledge and the skill to turn silver into gold, and copper and tin into silver. As a matter of fact, the one who has strong trust in God, is ahead of the alchemist in ten ways.

ONE: The alchemist needs certain chemical substances [and equipment] without which he cannot produce anything, yet these raw materials are not always available. But the livelihood of one who trusts in God, is always assured one way or another, as it says, *"This was to teach you that it is not by bread alone that man lives, but by all that comes out of the mouth of Hashem"* (Devarim 8:30). God does not lack ways to bring about ones livelihood. We know this from, (1) the story of Eliyahu [who had to hide in a cave] and was brought food by the ravens (I Melachim 17:4-6), and (2) from the story of the widow of Tzorfas [where miraculously the container of flour and pitcher of oil was always full](ibid. 17:9), (3) from that of the cake baked on coals and the pitcher of water [which sustained Eliyahu for forty days] (ibid. 19:6), and (4) from the episode of the prophets and Ovadyah who said, *"I hid a hundred men of the prophets of Hashem, fifty men to each cave, and sustained them with food and water"* (ibid. 18:13). It also says, *"Lions have been reduced to starvation, but those who turn to Hashem shall not lack any good"* (Tehillim 34:11), and *"Fear Hashem, you His holy ones, for those who fear Him lack nothing"* (ibid. v. 10).

TWO: The alchemist must do certain things and follow certain procedures in order to get results. He might even get killed in the process from all the [poisonous] fumes and vapors, coupled with both the never-ending work and the tremendous strain he is under around the clock. But one who trusts in God, is protected from harm, and his mind is at ease, for he is assured that no trouble will come his way. Whatever God brings him fills him with joy and happiness; he earns his livelihood with peace of mind, composure and tranquility, as it says, *"In lush meadows He lays me down, beside tranquil waters He leads me"* (ibid. 23:2).

THREE: The alchemist is afraid to reveal his secret formulae to anyone, for fear that he might be killed. But one who trusts in God, is not afraid of anyone. On the contrary, he is proud of his faith, as King David phrased it, *"In Hashem I have trusted, I shall not fear; what can man do to me?"* (ibid. 56:12).

FOUR: The alchemist is always caught in a bind. Either he stockpiles a large amount of silver and gold for when he needs it, or he puts away only enough to last a short while. If he carries a large stock, he lives in constant fear of losing it one way or another. He has no peace of mind. He is tense and nervous worrying that the king's agents might confiscate it or someone [might steal it]. On the other hand, if he carries only enough to last him for a short while, it may very well happen that when he urgently needs money, his supplies and ingredients run out. But the one who trusts in God, firmly believes that God will provide his livelihood according to His will, whenever and wherever He wishes, just as He nourishes the fetus in his mother's womb, the chick inside the egg where nothing from the outside can reach it, the bird in the air, the fish in the water and the tiny delicate ant. On the other hand even the strong lion at times cannot find any prey, as it says, *"Young lions want and hunger" (Tehillim 34:11)*. Furthermore it says, *"Hashem will not bring hunger upon the souls of the righteous" (Mishlei 34:11)*, and *"I have been a youth and also aged, but I have not seen a righteous man forsaken, nor his children begging for bread" (ibid. 37:25)*.

FIVE: The alchemist, [because of his fraudulent profession] lives in constant fear of everyone, from the king down to the plainest of people [who might denounce him]. But one who trusts in God is respected by kings and by the most influential people; even animals and inanimate stones want to do his will, as it says, *"Whoever sits in the refuge of the Most high . . ." (ibid. 91:1)* to the end of the psalm, [where the psalmist delineates the divine protection provided to the righteous], and *"From six troubles He will save you, and in the seventh no harm will reach you; in famine He will deliver you from death (Iyov 5:19,20)* until the end of the chapter.

SIX: The alchemist is not protected from illness and disease which may keep him from enjoying his wealth; he may not be able to delight in his possessions and derive pleasure from his achievements. But one who trusts in God, is safe from illness and disease, unless the sickness comes to atone [for a transgression] or to compensate for something.[1] As it says, *"Youths may weary and tire, and young men may constantly falter, but those whose hope is in Hashem will have renewed strength" (Yeshayah 40:30,31)*, and *"For the arms of the wicked will be broken, but the support of the righteous is Hashem" (Tehillim 37:17)*.

SEVEN: The alchemist may not be able to feed himself despite all his gold and silver, because occasionally, there will be a food shortage in his city. As it says, *"They will throw their silver in the streets, and their gold will become repulsive (Yechezkel 7:19)* and *"Even their silver, even their gold will not be able to rescue them" (Tzefaniah 17:19)*. But one who trusts in God, will never lack food as long as he lives, no matter where he is, as it says, *"In famine He will deliver you from death, and in war from the power of the sword" (Iyov 5:20)* and *"Hashem is my shepherd I shall not want" (Tehillim 23:1)* and, *"They will not be shamed in time of calamity; and in days of famine they will be satisfied" (Tehillim 37:19)*.

EIGHT: The alchemist cannot stay put in any one place for fear that his secret formula will be exposed. But one who trusts in God, will live safely and securely in his country, as it says, *"Trust in God and do good, dwell in the land and nourish yourself with faithfulness" (Tehillim 37:3)* and *"The righteous will inherit the earth and dwell forever upon it" (ibid. v. 29)*.

NINE: The alchemist cannot take his art with him to the hereafter, and in this world it only protects him from poverty and from dependence on others. But one who trusts in God will be rewarded for his trust both in this world and in the World to Come. For it says, *"He who trusts in Hashem, shall be surrounded with favor" (Tehillim 32:10)* and *"How abundant is the good that You have in store for those who fear You" (ibid. 31:20)*.

[1.] Such as to receive great reward in the World to Come, or to atone for his generation and to cancel an evil decree.

TEN: If the alchemist's occupation becomes public knowledge, his life is in jeopardy, because the things he does are against the laws of nature. And indeed if he does not keep his secret, the Almighty will designate [a judge or a ruler] who will condemn him to death. But people will admire and honor one who trusts in God. People will consider themselves lucky to be near him and to see him. He will raise the city's prosperity, and because of him the residents of the city will be protected from misfortune, as it says, *"A righteous one is the foundation of the world" (Mishlei 10:25)*. This can also be seen from the story of Lot [who found refuge in Tzoar and the city was saved from destruction because of Lot's presence] (Bereishis 19:19-23).

SERVING HASHEM WITH HAPPINESS

Trust in God is beneficial to one's observance of the Torah. If he is wealthy, he will quickly, eagerly and generously fulfill his financial obligations toward God and his fellowman. If he is poor, he will consider poverty as a favor from God, for it frees him from the obligations toward God and his fellowman, which money entails. Poverty also saves him the bother of safeguarding and managing his capital.

The story is told about a certain devout man who used to say, "I wish Hashem would save me from scattering my soul." People asked him, "What do you mean by 'scattering your soul'?" He replied, "Having investments in every port and every city, [because my financial worries distract me from serving God]." That is what our Sages had in mind when they said, "The more possessions a person has, the more worry he has" (Avos 2:7) and "Who is rich? He who is happy with his lot" (ibid. 4:1).

One who trusts in Hashem will attain the benefits of money namely, earning a livelihood, without the anxieties and constant irritations that plague a rich man. As Shlomoh Hamelech said, *"A worker's sleep is sweet, whether he has much or little to eat; but the rich man's abundance does not let him sleep" (Koheles 5:11)*.

Another benefit [of trusting in God] is that your wealth does not stand in the way of your faith, because you don't rely on your money. Rather, you consider your wealth, money that has been placed in your care to use for specific objectives and charitable purposes. [If you look at it this way,] even if you remain wealthy, you will not become arrogant. You won't boast of your kindness when giving charity, since you are only doing what you were ordered to do. You won't expect thanks or praise for your kindness, instead you will thank God for giving you the opportunity to do good deeds to others.

Then again, if you lose your money, you will not be upset and cry over it. Rather, you will thank God for taking back His deposit, just as you thanked Him when He handed it to you. You will be happy with what you have. You will never try to hurt anyone or envy anyone's wealth, as Shlomoh Hamelech says, *"A righteous person eats to satisfy his soul"* *(Mishlei 13:25)*—[meaning that after he has taken care of his needs he is satisfied and does not crave anything else.]

HAPPINESS AND JOY IN WORLDLY MATTERS

Trusting in God is also beneficial regarding worldly matters. To mention a few advantages:

□ You will be free from worldly cares, and will experience the tranquility that comes from curbing your physical desires. You will feel a sense of calmness, security and serenity, as it says, *"Blessed is the man who trusts in God, then Hashem will be his security. He will be like a tree planted near water which spreads out its roots along a brook"* *(Yirmeyah 17:7,8)*.

□ You won't feel the urge to go on long [business] trips to distant places. Such trips are exhausting and harmful to a person's health, as it says, *"He has weakened my strength on the way; He has shortened my days"* *(Tehillim 102:24)*.

The story is told, that a certain ascetic before assuming his ascetic life-style, traveled to a far off country to earn a living. On the way there, he met an idol worshiper from that city.

"How totally blind you all are!" said the ascetic. "How utterly stupid of you to worship idols!"

"So whom do you worship?" asked the idol worshiper.

"I worship the Almighty, All-Providing, All-Sustaining, the One and Only, Incomparable Creator," replied the ascetic.

"But your actions contradict your words," countered the idolater.

"How is that?"

"If what you say is true," said the idolater, "then He could have fed you at home just as easily as here. You wouldn't have to take the trouble to come all the way to this distant place!"

Caught off balance and unable to reply, the ascetic returned home where he took up asceticism and never left his hometown again.

□ If one trusts in God he will enjoy the peace of mind and the soothing calm that comes from not having to do hard and exhausting work, [because he realizes that God can provide for him without doing work that does not fit his constitution]. He will give up dangerous government jobs such as enforcing the law or collecting exorbitant and oppressive taxes.

One who trusts in God chooses an easy profession that will earn him a good reputation, offer him spare time to reflect and allows him enough time to study the Torah and fulfill all his religious obligations. He knows that nothing he does will either increase or lessen the amount of money he is destined to earn—it is completely dependent on God's decree—as it says, *"For what lifts a man up comes not from the east nor the west nor the wilderness. For God is the judge—He lowers one man and raises another"* (Tehillim 75:7), and *"In lush meadows He lays me down, beside tranquil waters He leads me"* (ibid. 23).

□ One who trusts in God has fewer frustrations in his business. He is not overly concerned when his product does not sell, when he cannot collect the money his creditors owe him, or when he becomes ill. He knows that God is wiser than he is, and He knows what is good for him better than he himself, as it says, *"Truly wait quietly for God, O my soul, for my hope comes from Him"* *(Tehillim 62:6).*

☐ A person who trusts in God is happy in whatever situation he finds himself, even if it is against his nature. He trusts that God does only what is good for him, like a loving mother who bathes, diapers, dresses and undresses her child, even though the child does not want it. As David said, *"I swear that I have stilled and quieted my soul, like a suckling child at his mother's side, like the suckling child is my soul"* *(ibid. 131.)*

List of Ideas Dealt with in the Coming Chapters

Now that I have expressed my thoughts about the benefits and advantages of trusting in God and its benefits as they relate to observing the Torah and attaining worldly pursuits, I will expand on seven points that concern this trust.

THE FIRST: The definition of trust.

THE SECOND: Qualities needed for one to be trusted.

THE THIRD: Fundamental beliefs necessary for one to trust God, and the need to actively seek a livelihood.

THE FOURTH: When one should display trust—when is it commendable, and when it is reprehensible.

THE FIFTH: The difference between how one who trusts in God and one who does not trust in God earn their living.

THE SIXTH: The need to denounce the view of people who have a "security mentality" and say they will begin to serve God only after they have enjoyed the pleasures of life.

THE SEVENTH: Factors that prevent one from trusting God;— additional points on this subject, and a brief overview.

CHAPTER ONE

THE DEFINITION OF TRUST

———⊙———

Trust is the feeling of confidence one has when he is sure that the one he trusts will do that which is advantageous for him, [do it] to the best of his ability, and knows what is good for him.

There is one basic element to trust without which there can be no trust: You must be confident that the one you trust keeps his word and does what he says. Furthermore, he will do things he did not promise and is not required to do, simply because he is good-hearted and kind.

CHAPTER TWO

QUALIFIES NEEDED FOR TRUST

———✦———

There are seven qualities one must have to be worthy of being trusted.

The First: The one you trust must be compassionate, sympathetic, and loving. For you will only trust someone and feel confident imposing upon him if he has compassion and sympathy for you.

The Second: You must be confident that in addition to his love, he will not overlook or ignore your wishes. Rather he will make every effort to carry out your request, and your concern is always on his mind.

If you have any doubts about this, and suspect that he might ignore or push aside your request you cannot fully trust him. On the other hand, if he is both compassionate and keenly concerned about your affairs, you can trust him implicitly.

The Third: He must be capable [of fulfilling your request] and not be overwhelmed by the task; nor should anything be able to prevent him from fulfilling it. If he were not equal to the task, you could not trust him, even were he compassionate and concerned with your affairs, because there are many things he simply could not do. But if he possesses all three qualities, [compassion, concern and capability], then he warrants your trust.

The Fourth: He must know what is inherently good for you, and be able to discern that which is truly good and that which only appears to be good.[2] Thereby he will do only those things that are truly good for you. You cannot feel confident placing your trust in him if he does not know these things. But if he has the aforementioned characteristics, then you can trust him without doubt.

The Fifth: You must be under his exclusive care from birth through infancy, childhood, adolescence, adulthood, old age until the end of your days. When you become aware of this, confidence in him will follow. You will rely on him, since he has already done so much for you in the past and is continuing to show you kindness all the time. This will cause you to trust him implicitly.

The Sixth: You must realize that you can trust and depend only on him for everything; no one else can harm you or help you, improve your situation or protect your from harm, like a servant imprisoned in his master's dungeon and completely under his master's domination. Under such circumstances you will surely trust him.

The Seventh: He must be completely, constantly and endlessly generous and kind to anyone, whether they deserve it or not. Someone who has these qualities, in addition to those mentioned previously, meets all the standards for trust. If you know such a person, it is your duty to trust him and to have confidence in him outwardly and inwardly, [and prove your trust] through your thoughts and actions. You should submit to him, accept his decrees, and judge all his decisions and actions favorably—[believing that they are for your own good, even if at times you are made to suffer].

These Criteria Are Found Only in God

If we analyze these seven requirements [for trust], we discover that human beings have none of them, but the Creator possesses them all.

---

2. Some things seem to be beneficial on the surface, but are essentially harmful. For example, a king promoted his friend to the rank of general, but because of his high rank he was captured by the enemy.

He has compassion for His creatures, as it says, *"Compassionate and gracious is Hashem" (Tehillim 103:8)*, and *"And shall I not take pity upon Nineveh the great city?" (Yonah 4:11)*.

He never ignores us, as it says, *"See, the guardian of Israel neither slumbers not sleeps" (Tehillim 121:4)*.

He is all-knowing and unchallenged, as it says, *"Wise of heart and mighty in power, who ever challenged Him and came out whole?" v 9:4)*, and *"Yours, Hashem, are greatness, might, splendor, triumph and majesty" (I Divrei Hayamim 29:11)*, and *"Hashem, your God, is in your midst, the mighty One who will save" (Tzefaniah 3:17)*.

He alone directs a person's life from the moment he is born and throughout his life, as it says, *"Is He not your Father, your Master, the One who made and established you?" (Devarim 32:6)*, and *"I relied on You from my birth, You withdrew me from the innards of my mother" (Tehillim 71:6)*, and *"You poured me out like milk, curdled me like cheese. . ." (Iyov 10:9)*.

Success and failure are not in the hands of man, but controlled by God alone, as it says, *"Whose decree was ever fulfilled unless the Lord willed it? Is it not at the word of the Most High that good and evil emanate?" (Eichah 3:37,38)*, and *"Grass withers and blossoms fade, but the word of our God stands forever" (Yeshayah 40:8)*, and *"Indeed the people are but grass" (ibid. v.7)*. This subject has been discussed extensively in the Gate of the Service of God.

God's generosity is boundless and His kindness all-encompassing, as it says, *"Hashem is good to all, and His mercy is on all His works" (Tehillim 145:9)*, and *"He gives nourishment to all flesh, for His kindness endures forever" (ibid. 136:25)*, and *"You open Your hand and satisfy every living being" (ibid. 145:16)*.

[There really is no need to cite all these verses] because common sense tells you that these seven criteria are found only in God and not in any human being. I only quoted the above [familiar] passages to help you remember [the seven criteria for trust].

When this becomes clear to you and you fully appreciate how truly kind God is, then you will trust in God, give yourself over to Him, let Him be your guide, never question His judgment and never grow angry at the difficult destiny He may choose for you. As David said, *"I will raise the cup of salvation, and in the Name of Hashem I will call"* (Tehillim 116:13), and *"Distress and grief I will find, then in the Name of Hashem I will call"* (ibid v. 3,4).

CHAPTER THREE

BELIEFS NECESSARY FOR ONE TO TRUST GOD

—————=◉=—————

Only if you are absolutely and fully convinced of five basic beliefs can you attain complete trust in God.

THE FIRST: You must believe and understand that the seven parameters necessary for trusting someone mentioned in the previous chapter and substantiated by Scriptural verse, are present in God.

To review and elaborate on these characteristics:

ONE: You must believe that the Creator has more compassion for you than anyone else has. Any compassion or mercy shown to you by others is only a reflection of God's compassion and mercy, as it says, *"[Hashem] will cause you to be compassionate and He will have compassion on you and multiply you" (Devarim 13:18).*

TWO: You must believe that God is aware of your needs and knows what is best for you. This stands to reason, for you are one of God's creations. No one knows what is good or bad for something, what can go wrong with it, how it might break and how to repair it better than the one who made it. If this is true of people who fashion material things—who do not really create [things] because they are incapable of creating essential matter rather only shape raw material into different forms—surely this is true of the Creator, who created man's essence, form, characteristics and composition. Without question, He knows and understands best what is good or bad for man, and what benefits him in this world and in the World to Come. As it says, *"I am Hashem your God, Who instructs you for your benefit, Who guides you in the way you should follow"* *(Yeshayah 48:17)*, and *"For Hashem admonishes the one He loves, and like a father He mollifies the child"* *(Mishlei 3:12)*.

THREE: You must believe that the Creator is the most powerful Being, that His promise is immutable and His decree irreversible, as it says, *"Whatever He pleases He does!"* *(Tehillim 115:3)*, and *"So shall be My word that emanates from My mouth; it will not return to Me unfulfilled"* *(Yeshayah 55:11)*.

FOUR: You must believe that God oversees the conduct of all people, that He neither forsakes nor ignores them; that nothing they do—small or great—escapes His attention, and that, while He focuses on one thing, His attention is not diverted by something else. As it says, *"Why do you say, O Jacob, and declare O Israel, 'My way is hidden from Hashem, and my cause has passed by my God'? Did you not know? Did you not hear? Hashem is the eternal God, the Creator of the ends of the earth; He does not weary, He does not tire; there is no calculating His understanding"* *(Yeshayah 40:27,28)*.

FIVE: You must believe that no one can help or hurt either oneself or anyone else without the Creator's consent. If a servant has many masters and each of them can help him, it is not sensible for him to rely on only one of them, because he expects each of them to help him. Of course, if one master had the ability to help him more than the others, he would depend on that one more than on the others—but to some extent he would still rely on the others. However if only one of his masters could help or hurt him, then he would trust that master alone, since he would not expect the others to help him.

So too, if you realize that nothing in the world can help or hurt you without the Creator's consent, you will not be afraid of people, nor place your trust in them. You will trust the Creator alone, as it says, *"Do not rely on nobles, nor on a human being, who cannot help"* *(Tehillim 147:3)*.

SIX: You should be aware of God's great kindness to you. Out of abundant kindness and goodness He created you, although you did not deserve to be created. He did not need to create you. He did it out of generosity, goodness and kindness, as we explained in the Gate of Reflection. For David said, *"Much have You done, O You, Hashem, my God; Your wonders and Your thoughts are for us. None can compare with You. Were I to relate or speak of them, they are too overwhelming to recount" (Tehillim 40:6).*

SEVEN: You should clearly understand that everything in this world, whether essential or accidental,[3] has a definite limit. Nothing can be added to or subtracted from what God has decreed regarding its quantity [i.e. its size], quality, [whether it is hard, soft, brittle, hot, cold], time or place. No one can enlarge what He made small, or reduce what He made large. By the same token, no one can delay an event God wants to hasten nor hasten an event He wants to delay. [If someone thinks that life experience appears to negate this and one can cause change by his actions, this is because he does not understand the true principles of cause and effect.]

THE LONG CHAIN OF CAUSE AND EFFECT

Whatever happens was preordained by Divine foreknowledge and came into being by means of a long chain of cause and effect. It appears to a person who does not understand the workings of the world that the cause that apparently brought about a change is in fact what brought it into being. The truth is, that this assumed cause is too weak and insignificant to bring about a change or modification in the essence of a thing.

Take a single grain of wheat, for example. It can produce three hundred ears of wheat, each of which contains another thirty grains of wheat. Thus, one single grain of wheat can produce close to ten thousand grains of wheat. Now, can anyone be so blind and fail to

---

3. Accidental and essential are philosophical terms. To say, for example, of an animal, that it is brown, or large, or hungry, is to give it accidental qualities at that moment. To say that it is a horse, is to state the one essential and permanent thing about it—its essence. The essence of anything is that which gives it continuous and independent existence.

recognize that one little grain, like any other planted seed, does not have the strength to produce such a huge quantity of grain?

The same is true for the procreation of man and other animals that develop from a drop of semen, as well as for the development of large fish from tiny fish eggs. [Obviously, the root cause is only from the will of Hashem].

Therefore, a person who, [in his eagerness to earn money,] goes to great lengths and expends vast energy and time, to make something happen before or after the Creator wants it to happen, or to make something either greater or smaller than the Creator wanted it to be, [does not understand that everything is ordained by God]. The only area proper to devote great energy and time to is in one's duty to serve God and accept His Torah; [for a person's moral character depends on his own choice.[4]] The person who worries and goes to great lengths to acquire his livelihood, reflects a lack of understanding of God's omniscience and reveals his ignorance of the benefits of God's guidance. Shlomoh Hamelech hinted at this when he said, *"Everything has its season, there is a time for every concern under the heaven" (Koheles 3:1)*. He then listed twenty-eight examples, including, *"A time to be born and a time to die"* until *"A time for war and a time for peace" (ibid. v. 2-8)*. He also says, *"But time and death will happen to them all" (ibid. 9:11)*, and *"For there is One higher than high who watches, and there are high ones above them" (ibid. 5:7)* [meaning, every event has a cause which, in turn, has a cause until the Primary Cause—Hashem]. The Creator's ways are so hidden, profound and elevated that man has no conception of any single action, much less can he understand Hashem's broader plan, as it says, *"As high as the heavens over the earth so are My ways higher than your ways, and My thoughts than your thoughts" (Yeshayah 55:9)*.

---

4. "Everything is in the hand of heaven except the fear of heaven" (Berachos 33b).

Preliminaries for Trust In God

[After reviewing the first requirement—the details necessary for trust mentioned in Chapter Two], we come to the second requirement for trust in God. This is, to be fully convinced that the Creator watches over you, that neither your deeds nor your thoughts are hidden from Him, and that He knows whether you trust Him sincerely or not. As it says, *"God knows the thoughts of man to be futile"* (Tehillim 94:11), and *"But the One who resides in hearts, He understands"* (Mishlei 24:12), and *"For You alone know the hearts of all people"* (1 Melachim 8:39).

Once you understand this clearly, you can no longer say you have faith in God unless you really trust Him with your heart and the essence of your being. Otherwise you would be like those about whom the verse says, *"With their mouths and their lips they honor Me, yet they keep their hearts far from Me"* (Yeshayah 29:13).

Trust Only in God

The third requirement for trust in God is, that you trust in God exclusively in all things and do not include anyone or anything else in your trust. If you include someone else in your trust, you ruin your trust in God. You know what it says about Asa when, in spite of his piety, he relied [on doctors rather than asking Hashem to cure him through the] doctors, *"In his illness he did not seek out Hashem, but only doctors"* (II Divrei Hayamim 16:12). He was punished for this.

It also says *"Blessed is the man who trusts in Hashem, then Hashem will be his security"* (Yirmeyah 17:7). Everyone knows that if two or more people are in charge of a job, it won't get done.[5] So it goes without saying that if a person trusts in God and at the same time in someone else, that his trust in God will be shattered. As a result,

---

5. "A pot in the charge of two cooks is neither hot nor cold" (Eiruvin 3a), or as the English saying goes, "Too many cooks spoil the broth."

the thing he wished for will not happen, as it says, *"Cursed is the man who trusts in man and makes flesh his strength and turns his heart away from Hashem"* (ibid. v.5).

DON'T BE A HYPOCRITE

The fourth requirement for trust in God is that you do your utmost to carry out the duties the Creator has imposed on you, observe His mitzvos, and stay away from the things He has forbidden. [You should fulfill your obligations toward God], just as you want God to provide you with the things for which you depend on Him. As our Sages put it, "Treat His will as if it were your own will, so that He will treat your will as if it were His will. Nullify your will before His will, so that He will nullify the will of others before your will" (Avos 2:4), and it says, *"Trust in Hashem and do good, dwell in the land and nourish yourself with faithfulness"* (Tehillim 37:3), and *"Hashem is good to those who trust in Him; to the soul that seeks Him* (Eichah 3:25).

How foolish and mindless is a person who trusts in God and at the same time rebels against Him. He must be empty-headed and ignorant! Doesn't he realize that if a person was ordered to either do something or refrain from doing something, and he disobeys that order, his employer will surely not keep his part of the bargain when he discovers this. This is all the more true if a person disobeys the laws and mitzvos of God. After all, God Himself warned that if a person defies Him, his hopes and aspirations will be dashed, and he will not deserve the title of "One who trusts in God." He will be like those of whom it says, *"What is the hypocrite's hope though he gains a profit, for surely God will cast away his soul. Will God heed his cry?"* (Iyov 27:8), and *"Can one steal, murder and commit adultery, swear falsely. . . and then come and stand before Me in this Temple upon which My name is proclaimed? Has this Temple upon which My name is proclaimed become a cave of criminals in your eyes?"* (Yirmeyah 7:9-11).

GOD IS THE PRIMARY CAUSE

The fifth requirement for trust in God is to understand clearly that ever since Creation, any new thing in this world came into being in one of two ways: either by a decree of the Creator or by means of direct or indirect causes, be they obvious or hidden. All these causes rush to bring the creation that God wants into being, and with God's help it becomes a reality.

To illustrate the meaning of direct and indirect causes let us examine a water wheel, where an animal turns a wheel that has buckets attached to it which bring water to the surface. The direct cause of the water being brought to the surface is the buckets. The indirect cause of this operation is the man who made the animal turn the wheel that brought up the water from the bottom of the well. The intermediate causes between the man and the buckets are the animal, the wheels and the rope. Now, if anything should go wrong with any of the parts between the man and the buckets, the entire operation [of drawing water] would come to a halt.

The same is true with any undertaking. Nothing in the world can succeed unless God decrees it and puts in place a series of causes that bring the enterprise to completion. For it says, *"The causes are measured by Him"* (I Shmuel 2:3), and *"Great in counsel and mighty in deed"* (Yirmeyah 32:19), and *"Hashem was the cause"* (I Melachim 12:15). If the in-between causes are missing, the natural processes cannot produce anything.

It is plain to see that it is necessary to work and expend effort in order to acquire a living. Let us say, a person is hungry, and food is placed in front of him. Unless he takes the trouble to lift the food to his mouth and chew it, he will never satisfy his hunger. Neither will he quench his thirst unless he picks up a glass of water and drinks it. Surely he must invest effort if he first has to prepare the food by grinding, kneading, baking, and the like, and even more so if he has to go out and buy the food and prepare it. He has to make an even greater effort if he does not have the money to buy the food, and has to earn it or sell some of his personal belongings.

WHY YOU MUST WORK HARD
TO EARN YOUR LIVELIHOOD

There are two reasons why the Creator wants man to work hard to earn a living. Firstly, because, God in His wisdom, thought it necessary to test man's soul to find out if he would serve God or rebel against Him. He devised a test that will reveal man's choice in this matter. The test consists of making man struggle to provide himself with things that are not essential to his soul, such as food, drink, clothing, shelter, and marital relations. He commanded him to go after them and obtain them in prescribed ways, with specific restrictions and at special times [in accordance with the laws of the Torah]. Those [material things] which God decides you should have, He makes available to you through various means. Those things He decides you should not have, He makes unobtainable to you.

That way, when you choose [the permitted things] or [the forbidden things] it becomes clear whether you want to serve God or transgress His laws. [By making a free choice[6]] you earn a reward [if you choose to do good], or punishment [if you choose evil], even if you do not carry out the [good or evil] deed.

The second reason [one must work hard to earn his livelihood] is because if a person did not have to work his fingers to the bone running after his daily bread, he would despise God and run after transgressions. He would not realize that he owes God for all the good He has done for him, as it says, *"They have a harp, a lyre, a drum and flute and wine at their drinking parties, but they would not contemplate the deeds of Hashem and would not look at the work of His hands"* (Yeshayah 5:12), and *"Jeshurun thus became fat and rebelled. You grew fat, thick and gross. [The nation] abandoned the God who made it, and spurned the Mighty One who was its support"* (Devarim 32:15). And as our Sages said, "Torah study together with an occupation is good, for the exertion you spend on both of

---

6. Without freedom of choice, reward and punishment would be meaningless.

them will make you forget sin. But Torah that is not joined with work will cease in the end, and leads to sin" (Avos 2:2). Surely this is true for a person who neither engages in Torah study nor an occupation.

As a matter of fact, God showed great compassion for man in keeping him busy all his life taking care of his needs in this world and preparing for the World to Come. This way he does not delve into things he does not need to know and cannot comprehend, such as; what happened before Creation and what will happen after the end. As Shlomoh Hamelech said, *"He has also put the needs of the world into their minds so that man cannot comprehend what God has done from beginning to end"* (Koheles 3:11).

But if you cherish the service of God, opt to fear God, trust Him in your Torah and worldly concerns, avoid shameful acts, set your sights on attaining good traits, are not disdainful of God when you are comfortable, don't choose leisure, aren't swayed by your evil impulse, and are not dazzled by the enchantments of the world— then the burden of having to earn a livelihood will be lifted from your shoulders. This is because the two aforementioned reasons for work, namely to test man's soul and in order that he not rebel when things are good, do not apply to you. You will earn enough to satisfy all your needs, without trouble and hard work, as it says, *"Hashem will not bring hunger upon the souls of the righteous"* (Mishlei 10:3).

WHY THE RIGHTEOUS SUFFER
AND THE WICKED PROSPER

Now if you may ask: We sometimes see righteous people who have to work very hard for a living, while many sinners live a life of ease, comfort and contentment. I will answer that the prophets and devout men have already probed this question. One of them asked, *"Why does the way of the wicked prosper?"* (Yirmeyah 12:1). Another said, *"Why do you allow me to see iniquity, and You look at evil deeds, with robbery and injustice before me, while the one who carries strife and contention still remains?" (Chavakuk 1:3)*, and *"For the wicked surround the righteous" (ibid. v. 4)*, and *"Why are you silent when the wicked swallows up he who is more righteous than he" (ibid. v.13)*, and *"Such are the wicked; ever tranquil, they amass wealth. . . It was for nothing that I kept my heart pure and washed my hands in innocence, seeing that I have been constantly afflicted and each morning brings new punishments" (Tehillim 73:12-14).* Another said about his generation, *"And so, we praise the wicked. . .they have even tested God and escaped" (Malachi 3:15).* Many more verses can be cited.

The prophet left this question unanswered. The reason for this is that the suffering of each righteous person is singular and no general rule can be made. So too with the tranquility of the wicked—the reason for each one is different. [Moshe] had this problem in mind when he said, *"The hidden things are for Hashem our God, but the revealed things are for us and our children forever" (Devarim 29:28).* The wise Shlomoh said in the same vein, *"If you see oppression of the poor, and the suppression of justice and right in the State, do not be astonished at the fact" (Koheles 5:7),* and as it says in the Torah, *"The Rock! Perfect is His work; for all His paths are justice" (Devarim 32:4).*

WHY RIGHTEOUS SUFFER

Nevertheless, I think it worthwhile for me to try to explain this problem, at least in a small way, to ease the mind of the troubled. A righteous man sometimes has to work very hard to earn a living and is put to the test, because of a sin he committed earlier in life that he must pay for now, as it says, *"Even a righteous person shall be punished on earth" (Mishlei 11:31).*

Sometimes [the righteous man has to suffer in this world] so that, in return, he will receive an infinitely greater reward in the World to Come, as it says, *"I have afflicted you and caused you hunger... to benefit you in the end" (Devarim 8:16).*

Sometimes he is caused to suffer to show the world his patience and his uncomplaining attitude in serving God, thereby setting an example for others, as we learn from the story of Iyov.

Sometimes God afflicts the righteous man because of the wickedness of his generation. He brings poverty and sickness on him [to atone for their sins] in order to demonstrate his piety and his [fervent] service of God, as it says, *"But in truth, it was our ills that he bore, and our pains that he carried" (Yeshayah 53:4).*

Sometimes he suffers because he was not zealous enough in taking up God's cause [and did not protest against the misdeeds] of the people of his generation, as we learn from the case of Eli [who shared his sons' guilt because he did not chastise them sufficiently], about whom it says, *"And it shall be that anyone left over from your family will come to bow down to him for a small coin or a loaf of bread" (I Samuel 2:36).*

WHY THE WICKED PROSPER

When God is kind to the wicked it may be because of a good deed the wicked man once did for which God rewards him in this world [with its fleeting material pleasures], as it says, *"He repays His enemies in their lifetime to make them perish [in the World to Come]" (Devarim 7:10),* which the early Sages [i.e. Targum Onkelos] translates as *"He repays His enemies during their lifetime for the good they did before Him, in order to destroy them."*

Sometimes good fortune is bestowed upon a wicked person in the form of a trust until God grants him a righteous son who will deserve it and inherit it, as it says, *"He prepares [the wardrobe] but a righteous man will wear it" (Iyov 27:17),* and *"To the sinner He has given the urge to gather and amass—that he may give it over to one who is pleasing before God" (Koheles 2:26).*

Then again, the wicked man's riches may not be a benefit to him at all; rather it may cause his downfall and actually kill him, as it says, *"There is a sickening evil which I have seen under the sun; riches hoarded by their owner to his misfortune" (ibid. 5:12).*

It may also be that the Creator endowed him with wealth to be used when he repents and becomes worthy of his good fortune, as happened with Menashe.[7] Or it may come to him as a reward for a favor his father did to someone, as it says about Yehu ben Nimshi, *"Four generations of your descendants will sit on the throne of Israel for your sake"* (II Melachim 10:30), and *"I have been a youth and also aged, but I have not seen a righteous man forsaken nor his children begging for bread"* (Tehillim 37:25).

Another reason God gives good fortune to the wicked is to test people who are deceitful and put up a false front. When they see the wicked prosper they will rush to curry favor with them, learn to act like them, and abandon the Torah way of life [thinking that they too, will become successful]. In the same vein, through the success of the wicked the righteous will be rewarded, when they continue to serve God in spite of being persecuted and humiliated by the successful evil people. They will be richly rewarded, as we know from the stories of Eliyahu with Izevel, and Yirmeyah with the kings of his generation [who both had to contend with evil rulers but by virtue of continuing on a righteous path were richly rewarded].

WHAT OCCUPATION SHOULD YOU CHOOSE?

Now that we have made it clear why it is our duty to actively pursue a livelihood, we want to point out that not everyone is obligated to go through the same process. There are many ways to earn a living. Some are easy and require little physical effort, like running a store, or light manual labor like sewing, embroidering, and barbering, or running a warehouse, supplying laborers or field workers. Other jobs require a lot of strenuous and tiresome labor, like tanning, mining iron and copper, refining silver by means of lead, carrying heavy loads, constantly traveling great distances, farming, plowing, and the like.

---

7. Menashe was an evil king who placed idols in the *Beis Hamikdash* and led the people astray. He was captured by the Assyrian army and taken to Babylonia. There he changed his ways and did *teshuvah*. Thereupon Hashem returned him to Yerushalayim and his kingship (II Divrei Hayamim 33:11-13).

If you are strong but of weak intelligence, you should choose a career that involves as much physical labor as you can handle. On the other hand, if you are physically weak but have a brilliant mind, you should not choose a profession that saps your strength, rather choose one which will be easy on your constitution and will enable you to be diligent in your studies.

Every person instinctively feels attracted to a certain profession or business because God implanted in him a love and proclivity for it. It is the same in the animal kingdom: a cat has the God-given instinct to catch mice, the hawk instinctively hunts the birds that nourish it, the instinct of certain predators tell them to hunt snakes, and some birds have the instinct to catch fish. In fact, God ingrained in every species of the animal world the craving for the particular plants or prey it needs in order to survive. The animal's body and its limbs are adapted to its needs. The birds that fish have long bills and legs, the lion has strong teeth and claws, the ox and the deer have horns. Conversely, animals that feed on grass and herbs do not have limbs suited for hunting and mauling.

In the same way, a person's qualities and physical makeup greatly influence his choice of profession or craft. If you find your personality pushing you toward a particular profession, and you are physically suited for it—you can bear its difficulties—follow that profession and acquire your livelihood that way. Accept willingly the difficulties that come with its pleasure. Don't be discouraged if you are out of work occasionally. Trust that God will provide for your livelihood all your life.

When you are busy physically and mentally earning a living, you should bear in mind that you are fulfilling the command of the Creator. For God commanded us to be involved in worldly pursuits, like farming, plowing and planting, as it says, *"Hashem took the man and placed him in the Garden of Eden, to work it and to guard it" (Bereishis 2:15).* God also commanded man to make use of all animals for his benefit and sustenance, to build cities, and to prepare food. He commanded him to marry and have marital relations with women in order to have children. [Being that working for a livelihood is in of itself serving God,] he will be rewarded because he had in mind to do these things for the sake of God with his heart and mind, regardless whether or not he reached his goal. As it says, *"When you eat the labor of your hands, you are praiseworthy and it is well with you"* *(Tehillim 128)*, and as our Rabbis said, "Let all your deeds be for the sake of Heaven" (Avos 2:17). If one does these things wholeheartedly for the sake of God, his trust in God will be complete, and the fact that he works for a living will not impair his faith in the least.

Don't think that your livelihood depends on one source only, and if that source dries up your income will stop. Trust God alone for your livelihood, and realize that to Him, all ways of earning money are the same. He will sustain you by whatever means, whenever and wherever He wants to. As it says, *"It is He who gives you the power to become prosperous"* *(Devarim 8:18)*, and *"Not by might nor by power, but through My spirit, says Hashem, Master of Legions"* *(Zechariah 4:6)*.

CHAPTER FOUR

WHEN TO TRUST GOD

<hr/>

An Analysis of Trust in the Creator.

There are two areas in which a believer should place his trust in the Creator:

ONE: To attain his needs in this world.

TWO: To acquire a portion in the World to Come.

His needs in this world can be further broken down:

ONE: Worldly needs that benefit his existence in this world.

TWO: Worldly needs that benefit him in the World to Come.

Worldly needs that benefit him in this world can be broken down into three categories: (1) those that benefit his body only; (2) those that help him earn a living, acquire wealth and accumulate resources; and (3) those that benefit his household, wife, relatives, friends and enemies, and people that are above and below him on the social ladder.

Worldly concerns that benefit him in the World to Come can also be further broken down: (1) All duties of the heart and those physical duties that apply only to him and neither hurt nor help anyone else and (2) physical duties that can only be fulfilled together with another person, where one is active and the other passive, like charity, acts of kindness, teaching, urging others to do good and warning against evil.

Matters of the World to Come fall into two categories; (1) reward that is earned [by good deeds in this world], and (2) reward that the Creator out of His grace grants to the pious and the prophets in the World to Come.

To sum up, there are seven areas in which you should trust the Creator:

1: Your own physical concerns.

2: Your wealth and sources of income.

3: Your wife, children, relatives, friends and enemies.

4: Duties of the heart and the physical duties that apply only to you.

5: Physical duties affecting others.

6: Reward in the world to come that is earned by good deeds in this world.

7: Reward in the World to Come which the Creator graciously grants to His treasured ones, as it says, *"How abundant is Your goodness that You have stored away for those who fear You, that You have performed for those who take refuge in You in the presence of men"* (Tehillim 31:20).

Since I explained [earlier in this Gate] the prerequisites for trusting in God, I find it my duty to continue with a point by point explanation of the proper way to trust in God—or anyone else—in each of these seven areas of trust.

I. TRUSTING IN GOD FOR YOUR PHYSICAL HEALTH

I will begin by highlighting the first area of trust in God which has to do with your own physical concerns, like life, death, your livelihood, clothing, shelter, health, illness, and character traits. The right way to rely on God in each of these areas is to surrender yourself to the fate that God decreed for you, and trust in Him. You should know that you only will have what the Creator meant you to have, and that will always be the best for you in this world and in the World to Come. You should also know that God completely controls all [your physical concerns], so that no one can advise you or bring about a change in them without God's permission.

Remember, no human being has the power to supply your sustenance, your clothing and other physical needs, any more than he
can make decisions about life and death, sickness and health.

Even while, on the one hand, you are fully convinced that everything you acquire is determined by the Creator, and that He chooses for you the best possible choice, you should, nevertheless, pursue a career and make decisions that seem to benefit you. God will
do [through your actions] what He decided to do.

Similarly, although your life span is determined by Divine decree, you still have to make an effort to earn a living in order to fill
your needs for food, drink, clothing and shelter. You may not leave
them to God and say, "If God wants me to live, He will sustain me
without food all my life, so why should I bother working to earn a
living?"

By the same token, you should not expose yourself to danger,
drink poison, fight lions or other wild beasts needlessly, jump into
the sea or into a fire, or do anything else unsafe and dangerous relying on God's decree [that you will live a set period of time]. The
Torah warns us about this, stating, *"Do not test Hashem, your God
as you tested Him at Massah" (Devarim 6:16).*

For if a person puts himself in danger, one of two things is
bound to happen to him: either he will lose his life [or he may be
saved through the grace of God]. Losing his life in this manner is
considered suicide and he will be held accountable [in the
Heavenly tribunal] as if he had killed someone—even though in
that case too death came about only through God's decree and
will. God warned us not to cause the death of any human being,
saying, *"Do not commit murder" (Shemos 20:13).* The closer the relationship between a murderer and his victim, the more severe is his
punishment, as it says, *"Because he pursued his brother with the sword
and suppressed all pity" (Amos 1:11).* Therefore, [since every person
is his own closest relative,] a person who kills himself surely will be
severely punished [in the hereafter]. He is like the servant whose
master ordered him to guard something for a while, warning him
not to leave until the master's messenger would relieve him. The
servant, seeing that the messenger was delayed in coming, left early.

[When the master found out,] he became furious and punished the servant severely. So too, a person who does not properly protect himself from harm turns his back on God's service and rebels against Him.

That is why, when [God commanded Shmuel to anoint David,] Shmuel said, *"How can I go? If Shaul finds out he will kill me"* (*I Shmuel 16:2*). This was not considered a lack of trust in God. In fact, God's reply to him indicates that Shmuel's wariness was commendable, for God [told Shmuel what pretext to use in order to avoid the dangerous confrontation with Shaul] and said to him, *"Take along a heifer, and say, 'I have come to bring an offering to Hashem'"* (*ibid*). Had Shmuel's statement stemmed from a lack of trust in God, God's answer would have been, *"I put to death, and I bring life, I struck down and I will heal!"* (*Devarim 32:39*). We find this when Moshe [tried to evade God's mission to redeem the Jewish people,] and said, *"I find it difficult to speak and find the right language"* (*Shemos 4:10*). God replied, *"Who makes a person dumb or deaf? Who gives a person sight or makes him blind? Is it not I—Hashem?* (*ibid. v. 11*).

If the perfectly righteous Shmuel hesitated to take the slightest risk, even though he was on a mission for God who told him, *"Fill your horn with oil and go forth, I will send you to Yishai the Bethlehemite"* (*1 Shmuel 16:1*) [to anoint his son as the successor to King Shaul], surely it would be shameful for a person not acting on God's orders to expose himself to danger.

Even if [the person who exposed himself to danger] was saved with God's help, he still loses his merits and forfeits his reward.

This principle of not relying on God in face of danger was formulated by our sages: "A person should never stand in a place of danger and say that a miracle will be performed for him, lest it is not. Even if a miracle is performed for him, it is deducted from his merits" (*Shabbos 32a*). As our forefather Yaakov said, *"I am unworthy of all the kindness"* (*Bereishis 32:11*), which the Targum translates, *"My merits are reduced by all the kindness and good."*

What we have said about life and death, [that although this is ultimately decided by God, one must nevertheless actively protect oneself from harm], applies also to matters of health, sustenance, shelter, acquiring good character traits, and avoiding bad ones. [While pursuing these goals,] you should bear in mind that your efforts in themselves are futile, you will receive only what God decrees. In that regard you must be like the farmer who plows his field, weeds, sows, and irrigates it, but ultimately must trust that the Creator will make the land fertile, protect it from disaster, increase its crop, and bless it. It would not be right for the farmer, [realizing that ultimately it is God Who causes crops to grow], to leave his field untilled and unplanted and rely on God to make things grow without his seeds.

In the same way, craftsmen, businessmen and laborers must earn a living while at the same time believing that their sustenance is in God's hands. He alone guarantees man his daily bread and gives it to him whatever way He chooses. One should not think that his efforts alone brought him his sustenance.

If you earn a living through your efforts don't depend on that effort as the source of your income. Don't get enthralled with your work or completely wrapped up in it, because that weakens your trust in God. Don't think that through your efforts you can earn more than God has allotted for you. Instead of taking pleasure in the fact that you are capable and have made successful arrangements, thank the Creator for providing you with a living after your toil, and that your hard work and trouble was not in vain. As it says, *"When you eat the labor of your hands, you are praiseworthy, and it will be well with you" (Tehillim 128:2).*

> Although it may appear that one's sustenance is dependent on another person, ultimately this is not true, it is completely in the hands of God.

A devout man once said, "I cannot understand how someone who gives something to someone else can boast about his generosity and expect to receive thanks. After all, he was only fulfilling the will of the Creator, who decreed that the recipient would acquire it. What baffles me even more, is how a person who earns his living from someone can become submissive to him, and compliment and flatter him. After all the provider was compelled [by God's decree] to provide for him."

> Because working is only to fulfill God's decree that man should work, and ultimately his livelihood comes from God, not by virtue of the effort he puts in, it is improper to think that a change in one's profession will bring about a change in one's fortune. If one was not successful it is only because God decreed it so. Changing one's profession will not help.

If one day you don't earn any money in your business or profession, that may be because you have already earned your day's allotment, or maybe it will come to you another way. In any case, if your profession suits your personality, physical strength, and status and does not contradict your religion, you should continue with that profession and not be negligent in your duties. At the same time, you should trust that God will not abandon you, nor detach or hide Himself from you. As it says, *"Hashem is beneficent, a stronghold on the day of distress, and mindful of those who trust in Him"* *(Nachum 1:7).*

The same goes for health and sickness. You should have faith in the Creator in this regard, but nonetheless always do your best to stay healthy by natural means. You should fight disease in the accepted way, as the Creator commanded, *"He must provide for his complete cure"* *(Shemos 21:19).* But don't think for a moment that the natural causes of health or disease help or harm you, ultimately everything comes with God's permission.

> Cure of diseases ultimately comes from Hashem. Man's intervention through medicines is only to fulfill God's command that he should do what he can to heal himself.

When you trust in God, He will heal you, at times through medication and at times without it, as it says, *"He gives an order and heals them,"* *(Tehillim 107:20).* He may even cure you with some-

thing that is usually harmful. We know this from the story of Elisha
and the bad waters. It says, *"The water is bad, making the land
deadly" (II Melachim 2:19)*, Elisha cured it by throwing in salt
[which should have made the water totally undrinkable, and unfit
for human consumption]. So too we find, *"[God] showed [Moshe]
a tree. [Moshe] threw it into the water, and the water became drink-
able" (Shemos 15:25)*. The early rabbinic Sages commented that this
was an oleander tree,[which is poisonous but nevertheless it sweet-
ened the water.] The same idea is expressed here: *"Let them lift a
cake of figs and smear it on the abscess, and it will heal" (Yeshayah
38:21)*. You also know, of course, that Asa died because he relied
on the physicians to cure his sickness rather than on God (II
Melachim 16:12). And finally it says, *"For He inflicts pain and ban-
dages it, He crushes and His hands heal" (Iyov 5:18)*.

II. How Hard One Should Work to Earn a Living

The second area in which you should trust God involves your possessions, your sources of income, and the way you earn a living.
This includes a businessman, craftsman, commercial traveler, man-
ager, laborer, government employee, accountant, contractor,
banker, scribe, one who travels through deserts or crosses the seas,
and any other profession people engage in to amass money and be
able to indulge in life's luxuries.

The proper way to have faith in God in these matters is to do
the kind of work that God chose for you [by providing you with
specific talents, intellect and physical strength], and to earn enough
money to fill your basic needs. If God decides you should earn
more than that, it will come without trouble or hard work, provided you have faith in Him; go about your business, but don't rely
[on your profession] too much. If, on the other hand, God ear-
marked for you no more than the bare minimum, then, even if you
move heaven and earth to increase your wealth, you could not do
so. If you put your faith in God, you will find tranquility and inner
peace, because you know that the share that is allotted to you can-

not be turned over to someone else, nor will it come earlier or later than its appointed time.

THREE PITFALLS ONE WHO SUPPORTS OTHERS SHOULD AVOID

Sometimes God has a number of people derive their livelihood through an individual. This tests the benefactor to determine whether [in his affluence] he will continue to serve God or rebel against Him. This is one of the most difficult tests and temptations a person can face. This situation can be compared to a king who has to provide for his army and his servants. His generals, ministers, governors and their underlings have servants, attendants, clerks, wives and relatives [they have to support], and do not care whether they raise the money by honest or dishonest means.

The foolish [benefactor] is liable to make three mistakes:

> All that a person acquires is decided by Hashem. Even that which he acquires through dishonest means, is only his because Hashem willed it. That being the case he could have acquired the same amount through honest means.

The first one: He uses shameful and crooked means to get money that the Creator set aside for him. Had he used legal ways, he would have the same amount without violating the principles of the Torah and ethics, and would not lack anything the Creator had destined for him.

The second mistake is: He thinks that all the money he earns is for his own livelihood, [and that which he gives to others is his gift to them]. He does not understand that there are three types of income. The first is the income for one's own livelihood, meaning, food for his basic sustenance that God guarantees to every living creature [as our sages said "He who gives life gives sustenance" (Taanis 8b]. The second, is the income for the needs of others, for example one's wife, children, servants, attendants and the like. God does not guarantee this to everyone. Only a select few, [who are worthy of it], are guaranteed this; and then only under certain conditions and special circumstances; sometimes it happens, and sometimes not, depending on the dictates of the Creator's kindness and justice. [This is to say that not everyone is given the opportunity to be a master of servants, or a ruler of a city or country. For the few individuals who attain this position it is a test. If they help others, they earn a place in the World to Come; if they oppress their subjects they incur Heavenly punishment.] The third, is the income that is accumulated wealth. This money is of no use to the owner. He watches it and guards it until he leaves it to someone else or loses it. The fool thinks that all the money made available to him by the Creator is meant for his own sustenance and nourishment, so he rushes and works day and night to hoard the riches that may eventually go to his widow's next husband, his stepson, or his greatest enemy.

The third mistake [the foolish benefactor] makes is: He provides others with a livelihood, as the Creator decreed he should, then brags about how generous he is, as if it were he who actually supports and sustains them and is generous to them. Furthermore, he expects them to thank him and praise him extravagantly for it, and be subservient to him. He becomes conceited and gloats with inflated pride. He completely forgets to thank God [for making him the instrument to bestow kindness on others]. He believes that if he did not support them, he could keep this money for himself. He also thinks that, if not for him, they would be without an income. This poor misguided fellow is working in vain in this world and loses his reward in the World to Come.

But the intelligent person acts the proper way in accordance with the Torah and the ways of the world in all of these situations. [He earns an honest living. If he is wealthy, he gives charity, and does not boast of his benevolence or expect gratitude for it, but praises God for affording him the opportunity to help others.] He trusts that God is better able to provide him with a living and with possessions than he himself could be trusted to provide. He realizes that he does not know whether his wealth is for support and sustenance, or as capital [that will end up in the hands of others]. His conduct earns him honor in this world and a great reward in the World to Come, as it says, *"Praiseworthy is the man who fears Hashem, who greatly desires His commandments etc." (Tehillim chap. 112).*

THE FALLACY OF RESPECTING PEOPLE FOR THEIR WEALTH

There are people who go to great lengths to earn a lot of money solely so that others should look up to them. They love honor. They are never satisfied. [The more money they have, the more they want to accumulate]. They don't understand what brings real honor in this world and the next. They are misled when they see the common people admire the rich. [The reason common people respect the wealthy is] because they hope to acquire some of their riches themselves, or they hope to receive handouts from the wealthy.

If people would only realize that the wealthy have neither the ability nor the power to give or withhold anything without a decree from the Creator, they would not put their hopes on anyone except God. They would honor only a person whom God has endowed with outstanding qualities and therefore deserves honor, as it says, *"For I honor those who honor Me" (I Shmuel 2:30).*

> The wealthy believe that their great wealth comes on account of the energy they expend acquiring it. This is not so. They are wealthy because Hashem has so decreed. That being the case, they should spend their time and energy on the service of Hashem and their wealth will come without effort.

Because the wealthy are honored by the common people—who lack understanding of what truly deserves honor—the wealthy begin to believe that they deserve honor. Therefore, the Creator makes it more difficult for them; they end up expending vast energy and time to acquire their wealth, instead of striving to do what they should be doing, namely, fulfilling their obligations toward the Creator and thanking Him for all the good He did for them. Had they done this, their prospects would have been far better. For it says, *"Length of days is at its (the Torah's) right; at its left, wealth and honor"* (*Mishlei 3.16*) and furthermore it says, *"Wealth and honor come from You"* (*I Divrei Hayamim 29:12*).

WEALTH COMES FROM GOD

Some people who amass money acquire it through great toil and effort while others inherit it. Those that expend great energy, believe their effort brought them their wealth, and without their effort they would not achieve it. They praise the factor, [i.e. their business or job], rather than the actual cause [i.e. God].

We can compare them to a man who was wandering through the desert, tired and terribly thirsty. He came upon a well containing brackish water, and happily quenched his thirst. Further on, he found a well overflowing with fresh, sweet water. Now he was sorry he had drunk his fill from the water he had found earlier. So too, a rich man who acquired his wealth through [difficult and bitter] means should realize that, if he did not choose that particular source he could be just as rich from an easier profession, as we explained earlier. As it says, *"Nothing prevents Hashem from saving, whether through many or through few"* (*1 Shmuel 14:6*).

TRUSTING IN GOD FOR ONE'S LIVELIHOOD

One who trusts in God for his livelihood and finds himself one day without an income, should say to himself, "He who brought me into this world at a particular time—not a second earlier or later—

is now holding back my livelihood for a specific period of time, and He knows what is best for me."

[One who has been a man of means], and can now afford nothing beyond his basic personal needs, should say to himself, "Early in my life, God provided me at my mother's breasts with just enough food for each day and subsequently He advanced me to better things, until eventually I acquired wealth. Just as my mother's milk which came in small quantities, to fill my immediate needs, did not harm me, so too, I will suffer no harm with the limited income He gives me now, even if this situation continues for the rest of my life."

He will be rewarded for [being content with his basic needs], as our ancestors who were content with the measure of *manna* in the wilderness, as it says *"Let the people go out and pick each day's portion on its day"* (*Shemos 16:4*), were rewarded by the Creator. He said about them *"Go out and call in the ears of Jerusalem, saying, 'I recall the kindness of your youth. . .your following Me into the wilderness, into an unsown land'"* (*Yirmeyah 2:2*).

If a person's livelihood comes through working at a profession [he dislikes] or in a place [he dislikes] or for an employer [he does not care for], he should say to himself, "[God] created me in a specific form and image, and with specific qualities which are in my best interest. So too, He has determined that my livelihood should come in this specific way because it serves my interests best. It was He who brought me into this world in a particular place, and through two particular people. He decided that I should earn my living in this particular place and through this particular individual, all for my own good." As it says, *"Hashem is righteous in all His ways"* (*Tehillim 145:17*).

III. TRUST IN GOD CONCERNING FAMILY AND ASSOCIATES

The third area in which one must trust God is regarding one's wife, children, family relatives, friends, enemies, colleagues, acquaintances, and those who are above and below his status on the social ladder. I will point out the proper way of relying on God in these situations.

Everyone is in one of two situations: either he lives alone or amongst family and relatives. If you live alone and feel forlorn, God will be your companion. When you trust in Him, [you will find consolation] when you think how out of place and lonely every soul [which is purely spiritual] must feel in this [physical] world. Essentially all people in the world—[even those who have families]—are out of place. For it says, *"You are strangers and temporary residents with Me" (Vayikra 25:23).*

Reflect also on the fact that even one who has relatives, will eventually end up [in the grave where he is] alone, and neither a relative nor a son can help him or keep him company. Furthermore, you can take comfort in the fact that [by living alone] you are relieved from the heavy burden and obligation of supporting a family. You should consider this as a favor from the Creator. For if you are occupied with worldly matters, you won't have to work so hard to support a family. Not having a wife and family will make your life more relaxed and easier. And if you spend your time preparing for the afterlife, your mind undoubtedly will be clearer and more free when you are able to go into seclusion [to meditate]. It is for this reason that ascetics left their families and homes and retreated into the mountains—in order to free their minds for God's service. So too, the prophets, in order to contemplate their duties toward the Creator, would leave their homes and go into seclusion when the spirit of prophecy came upon them. We know this from the episode where Eliyahu met Elisha, as it says, *"He came upon Elisha the son of Shafat while he was plowing, twelve pairs of oxen were going before him, he being with the twelfth" (I Melachim 19:19).* As soon as Eliyahu gave him a slight hint, Elisha understood it and said, *"Please let me kiss my father and mother, and then I shall follow you" (ibid. 20).* The next verse says, *"He followed Eliyahu and served him" (ibid. 21).*

There is a story about an ascetic who went to a city to teach its inhabitants how to serve God. He discovered that everyone's clothing and jewelry were the same color. He noticed graves at their front doors, and that there were no women among them. He asked them the meaning of all this.

The people told him, "Our clothing are all similar so that no one can tell the difference between the poor and the rich; the rich will not become conceited and arrogant, and the poor will not be ashamed of themselves. In this manner the rich man will realize that his situation on earth is the same as his situation in the grave [where rich and poor are equal]." [They continued,] "We once had a king who would mingle with his servants. No one recognized him because he dressed very humbly and wore only the plainest jewelry."

"We placed the graves of our deceased relatives by our front doors," they explained, "to serve as a reproof, [and to remind us] to be ready for death, and to prepare provisions [of good deeds] that will get us to our final resting place [in the World to Come]."

"Regarding your observation that we separate ourselves from our wives and children," they clarified, "you have to realize that we set aside a settlement near here [for them]. We go there to take care of their needs whenever it is necessary. Then we return to this place. We do this because we noticed how distracted we became, and how much [time] we lost and how much pressure and tension we were under when our families were close to us—and how relaxed we were when they were away from us. Now we have the inner peace to focus on the concerns of the World to Come and to turn away from worldly matters."

The ascetic liked what he heard. He blessed them and commended them on their way of life.

DEVOTION TO FAMILY AND FRIENDS

If one who trusts God has a wife, relatives, friends and enemies, he must trust that God will save him from [being overburdened by their demands]. He must do his best to fulfill his obligations to them, do what they ask of him, and be sincere with them. He must not cause them any harm; he must do whatever he can to make them happy. He must be faithful in all things, and teach them to advance in Torah and worldly matters in order to serve God. For it says, *"Love your neighbor as [you love] yourself"* (*Vayikra 18:18*), and it says, *"Do not hate your brother in your heart"* *(ibid. 19:17).*

[Don't do kind things for your loved ones] in order to receive reward or to be repaid by them later on, or because you love being honored and praised by them, or because you want to make them subservient to you. Your only purpose should be to fulfill the Creator's commandments, to keep His covenant, and to observe His ordinances. If you do what your loved ones ask of you for the [selfish] reasons mentioned above, you will not get what you hoped for in this world; you will have labored in vain, and furthermore forfeit your reward in the World to Come.

On the other hand, if your intent is to serve God, God will reward you in this world, by putting your praises in [your loved ones' mouths] and making them respect you. He will also grant you great reward in the World to Come. As God said to Shlomoh, *"Even that which you did not request I have granted you—even riches and honor"* *(I Melachim 3:13).*

Concerning people higher or lower than you on the social ladder, the way to trust in God is this: if you have a request from one of them, rely on God [to fill your need]. Consider these people only as the messengers who are fulfilling His will, just as the farmer who tills the soil and plants for a living, knows that only if God decides he should be supported will the seeds sprout, produce fruit and increase. He knows that the soil does not deserve thanks, rather he is grateful to the Creator. If the Creator does not want to support him through the land, it will not sprout, or the crops will get ruined. He surely would not blame the land for that.

So too, when you ask someone for a favor, it should make no difference whether the person is strong or weak. Trust that God will enable you to attain your request. If the person fulfills your request, thank God for fulfilling it, and thank the person through whom the favor was fulfilled for his willingness and for having been chosen as God's instrument, for everyone knows that the Creator brings about good things only through good men, and rarely causes loss through them. As our Sages put it, "Merit is brought about through a person of merit, and punishment through a person of guilt" (Shabbos 32b), and as Scripture says, *"No harm befalls the righteous"* *(Mishlei 12:21).*

If the person does not fulfill your request, don't hold it against him, and accuse him of callousness. Rather, thank God for choosing what was best for you, and praise the person for trying to fulfill your wish, although it did not work out. This is how you should act with your friends, business associates, employees and partners.

If someone of higher or lower station in life makes a request from you, make a sincere effort to carry out his wishes, provided the one who asks is worthy of the effort. And trust God to help you accomplish it.

If, with God's help, you fulfilled his wish, and brought him great benefit, do not boast about it, or ask for thanks or renumeration. Rather, thank God [for making you His instrument]. If you tried but were unable to fulfill his request, don't feel bad about it. Simply tell your friend that you did your best, but could not carry it out.

How to Deal with Enemies

As for enemies and people who envy you or wish you harm, trust Hashem to deal with their animosity. Endure their insults, and don't retaliate against them. Repay them with kindness, doing as much good for them as you can. Keep in mind that the Creator alone has the power to help or harm you.

If your enemies brought hardship upon you, judge them favorably. Attribute your suffering to your own wrongdoings against God, and beg His forgiveness for your sins. If you do so, your enemies will come to love you, as the wise Shlomoh said, *"When Hashem favors a man's ways, even his foes will make peace with him"* (Mishlei 16:7).

IV. Faith and Free Will

The fourth area which people must trust in God has to do with the duties of the heart and with duties to Hashem that you fulfill with your body that affect you alone. This includes things like fasting, praying, *sukkah, lulav, tzitzis,* observance of Shabbos and the festivals and avoiding transgressions. All duties of the heart are also included because they have no effect on others.

Let me explain the right way to trust God in these matters. I ask God to guide me toward the truth, in His mercy. It is only possible to fulfill a mitzvah or transgress a negative commandment after having done three things: first, you must make a moral decision; second, you have to set your mind to follow through on that choice; and third, you have to take action to implement the chosen plan and make it a reality.

[Two of these three things are under your control, namely:] you are free to make the choice to serve God or to disobey him, and you are free to determine to follow through on that choice. It would be wrong and foolish to trust God that He instill in your heart the choice to do mitzvos, for the Creator left the *choice* of serving Him or rebelling against Him up to you. For it says, *"Choose life" (Devarim 30:19).* But whether you actually do the good or evil deed, is not up to you. That is dependent on things beyond your control, which are sometimes available and at other times not[8].

If you rely on God when faced with the choice of serving Him, and say you will not choose to do anything until He decides what is best for you, you will have strayed from the right way and abandoned the true path. For the Creator has commanded you to choose to serve Him, and pursue His service with energy and determination, sincerely for the sake of His great Name. He let us know that this is the proper way for us, both in this world and in the World to Come.

If after deciding to do Hashem's command you succeed and actually fulfill the commandment, you will be richly rewarded for making the decision to serve Him, for deciding to carry it out, and for the actual act done with your limbs. Even if you are unable to carry it out, you will be rewarded for making the choice and for

---

8. For example, you have the freedom to choose to get up in the morning to *daven.* It is also up to you to follow through on this by setting your alarm clock to wake you up. But you have no control over whether you actually will be able to get up in time. Your alarm may malfunction, you may not feel well, and many other factors may prevent you from carrying out your chosen course of action.

deciding how to carry it out, as we pointed out earlier. The same is true regarding punishment for transgression.

TRUST IN REGARD TO SERVING GOD AND REGARDING MATERIAL PURSUITS

The difference between serving the Creator and engaging in material pursuits, as far as trusting in God is concerned is, that concerning material things, you never know whether [the profession or business you choose] is good and helpful for you or whether it is detrimental and harmful. You don't know which vocation is most suitable for earning your livelihood and for maintaining your health and general well-being. You are in the dark as to what merchandise to carry, what sales technique to use, and what steps to take in order to be successful.

Therefore, when making decisions concerning which path to take in attaining a livelihood and how to carry it out, trust God to help you decide what is good for you. Do your best to achieve it and implore God to inspire you to make the right choices.

But the service of God is different. He has already outlined the right course to take and commanded us to choose it. He also guaranteed us a reward for following it. This being so, if you beg Him to help you make the right decision, [as you should do when making a living], and trust Him to show you what is good for you, your pleadings are misguided and foolish. He has already taught you how to serve Him in the way that will benefit you in this world and in the World to Come. For it says, *"Hashem commanded us to keep all these rules. . . for our own good, to give us life, as this very day"* (*Devarim 6:24*). And it says about the reward in the World to Come, *"And it will be a merit for us if we are careful to keep this entire mandate"(ibid. v.25)*.

Consider this also, often a business or vocation that on the surface seems profitable may prove a failure, and one that does not seem profitable turns out to be successful. But this is not so when it comes to serving God or transgressing His laws. There, what is contemptible or commendable is fixed and not subject to change.

[While you should not trust in God to make moral choices,] you should trust in Him to help you carry out an intended act of service to Him. [God will help you,] provided you have made the choice to do it wholeheartedly and sincerely, for the sake of His great Name. At this point it is your duty to implore Him to help and guide you, as it says, *"Lead me in Your truth and guide me . . . to You I have hoped all the day"* (Tehillim 25:5), *"Lead me on the path of Your commandments, for that is my desire (ibid. 119:35), "I have chosen the way of faithfulness" (ibid. v. 30), "I have clung to Your testimonies, O Hashem, put me not to shame" (ibid. v. 31)* and, *"Do not remove from my mouth the word of utmost truth, because I have yearned for Your ordinances" (ibid. v. 43).*

These verses prove that after the psalmist made the decision to serve God, he prayed for two things: The first, that God help him focus his thoughts and strengthen his determination by keeping worldly troubles from his heart and eyes, as it says, *"Let my heart be undivided in reverence for Your name" (Tehillim 86:11), "Unveil my eyes, that I may perceive wonders from Your Torah" (ibid. 119:18), "Avert my eyes from seeing futility" (ibid. v. 37), "Incline my heart toward Your testimonies" (ibid. v. 36),* and the like. And the second [thing the psalmist prayed for was], that God give him the physical strength so that his intentions to serve Him become a reality, as it says, *"Lead me on the path of Your commandments" (Tehillim 119:35), "Sustain me that I may be saved" (ibid. v. 117),* and many similar Scriptures.

In due time, with God's help, I will explain the concepts that negate these feeling, to set them straight, and the right course to follow in this regard.

V. DUTIES THAT INVOLVE OTHERS

The fifth area in which one must trust in God applies to physical obligations that involve others, such as charity, tithing, teaching wisdom, urging others to do good and warning them away from evil, returning money or borrowed items, keeping secrets, speaking well of others, doing favors, honoring parents, leading those who have gone astray back to God, teaching people about God's goodness, pitying the poor and having compassion for them, swallowing insults [which are hurled at you] when you prod people to serve God, offering them reward [for doing what is right], and frightening them with punishment [for transgressing].

The right way to trust God in these matters is to think them over carefully in your heart and resolve to do them. Then make plans to carry out these duties, as we mentioned above when we discussed man's duties to the Creator in the fourth [of the seven] areas in which people must trust in God.

You are required to do these things because they draw you closer to God. Don't do them in order to make a name for yourself and gain the respect of others, or for reward and power.

Trust that God will help you complete the task you have set for yourself, since He wishes this to be done.

Be careful to keep [your good deed] hidden from those who need not know about it. The reward of your deed will be greater if it is done secretly rather than openly. If you cannot hide it [and will receive honor or praise from the recipient], don't come to depend on this honor. Remember instead the principle we mentioned earlier, that no one in the world can help you without the will of the Creator.

When the Creator gives you the opportunity to do a mitzvah, consider it as if you were granted a favor. Don't exult with the praise you receive for fulfilling it, and don't look for honor and glory. That will make you boast about your good deed and taint the purity of your thoughts and intentions. It would cheapen your deed and diminish your reward [because the pleasure of receiving honor and adulation is considered part of your reward]. I will explain all this in the appropriate Gate, with God's help.

VI. Reward in This World and the Next

The sixth area in which one must trust God is concerning the reward in this world and the World to Come that one earns through his good deeds in this world. Reward can be given entirely in this world or entirely in the World to Come. Sometimes one deed can earn you reward in this world and the next.

Although this concept has not been fully explained to us, the Creator has promised His people reward for observance. He did not specify the reward in this world for fulfilling positive commandments, unlike the transgressions where He specified punishment in this world. We find transgressions that call for stoning, burning, decapitation, strangulation, forty lashes, death, *kares*—premature death, paying double, paying fourfold and fivefold, and paying for torts. This includes damages cause by an ox that gored or an animal that ate, a pit, a fire, wounding, seizing someone's private parts, slander and the like.

There are several reasons why the prophet [Moshe] told us nothing about reward and punishment in the World to Come in the Torah. First, because we know nothing about the nature of the soul without the body, much less what pleases or distresses it. God did explain the concept of reward in the World to Come to people who would understand the idea. For example, He said to Yehoshua, [the *Kohen Gadol*], *"I will permit you to move among these [angels] who stand here"* (Zechariah 3:7). This surely does not refer to [life in this world] when his soul was joined to his body. Rather it alludes to the afterlife when the soul, in its sublime and incorporeal state, is free of the body and takes on the form of an angel, once it is purified and radiant as a result of the good deeds it performed in this world.

Another reason [why there is no explicit mention in Scriptures of reward and punishment in the World to Come] is that the concept of reward and punishment in the World to Come was revealed to the common people by the prophets and the sages were able to come to this understanding through their own logical reasoning. It was not mentioned in Scriptures, just as the details of many mitzvos and other obligations were never written down. [The prophets] relied on the oral tradition [for this knowledge to be disseminated].

Also, [the Torah did not mention reward in the World to Come] because the common people [at the time of the giving of the Torah] were ignorant, as can easily be seen in the Torah. [The people worshiped the golden calf, craved meat, complained about the manna, rebelled against Moshe, sent the spies and displayed a lack of understanding of their mission (Pas Lechem)]. The Creator acted like a father who loves his child. When he has to discipline him, he feels sorry for him and is less harsh with him, as it says, *"When Israel was a lad, [i.e. when the nation was only a "lad" in Egypt], I loved him"* (Hoshea 11:1).

If a father wanted to teach his young and immature son knowledge as a prerequisite for esoteric concepts, he would not tempt him by saying, "If you just bear with the hard work and the tough studies, you'll reach the highest levels of learning." The child would not pay attention to his father because he would not recognize the value of the reward.

However, if the father promised his son something that gave instant gratification, such as food or drink, nice clothes, a nice wagon, or the like, or if he threatened him with something that gave him discomfort, like hunger, taking away his clothes, hitting him, or the like, and also stimulated him with convincing proofs and arguments backed by concrete facts, it would be easier for the child to accept the hard work and the tough lessons. As the boy grew and his mind ripened, he would understand the lessons his father taught him, and he would follow in that path. [In retrospect,] the sweet rewards that motivated him in the beginning would seem trivial to him. [He realizes now] that they were given only as inducements.

So too, the Creator promised His people an immediate reward or punishment. He realized that as soon as they would be ready to serve Him, they would shake off their misconception that reward and punishment in this world [is in itself the goal] and would resolve to serve Him for His sake. The same can be said of all the passages that describe God in corporeal terms [like, God saw, heard, came down, sits on a Throne, was standing on the ladder, the hand, eyes, mouth of God etc. The purpose of these metaphors is to help the common people understand the abstract metaphysical concepts they represent.]

Another reason [why reward in the World to Come is not mentioned] is that man can not earn reward in the World to Come solely as a result of his good deeds. He must add to his actions one of two things in order to earn this reward: Firstly, he must teach people how to serve the Creator and guide them to do good, as it says, *"Those who teach righteousness to the multitudes will shine like the stars for ever and ever"* *(Daniel 12:3)*, and *"The reprovers should be pleasant, and a good blessing will come upon them"* *(Mishlei 24:25)*. When the merits you have earned for making others righteous combine with the merits of your own righteousness, faith, and acceptance of your lot, you will deserve a reward in the World to Come in the eyes of the Creator.

Secondly [you receive reward in the World to Come] as a favor and an [unearned] gracious gift from God, as it says, *"And Yours, O Lord, is kindness, for You repay each man according to his deeds"* *(Tehillim 62:13)*. The reason [that God bestows His beneficence only out of His infinite kindness] is, because even were a person's good deeds as numerous as the sand of the sea, they would still not match a single one of God's great kindnesses to him in this world; how much more so if he has transgressed. If the Creator kept an account of the gratitude owed Him for His kindness, your good deeds would be offset and canceled by the smallest favor God did for you. Thus any reward the Creator bestows on you for your deeds is a gracious gift from God. Punishment on the other hand in this world and the next is based on truth and justice. There is therefore a debt each person must pay, but God's kindness hovers over us [and protects us] in both worlds, as it says, *"Kindness, O Lord, is Yours"* *(Tehillim 62:13)*, and *"Nevertheless, He, the Merciful One, is forgiving of iniquity and does not destroy"* *(ibid. 78:38)*.

There is another reason [why the concept of reward and punishment in the World to Come is not mentioned]. There are two kinds of good deeds: hidden ones, that only the Creator knows about, such as the duties of the heart and the like, and visible ones that are not hidden from others, like mitzvos you do with your limbs, [for example, *tefillin, tzitzis, lulav, sukkah, matzah,* and lighting Shabbos lights]. The Creator repays visible good deeds with rewards that are visible in this world, and He repays hidden, inner, good deeds with hidden rewards in the World to Come. That is why David described [the reward in the World to Come] as "hidden", stating, *"How abundant is Your goodness that You have hidden away for those who fear You" (Tehillim 31:20)*, [and fearing God is one of the duties of the heart—a hidden good deed]. The same is true of punishment for visible and hidden transgressions. Proof of this can be found in God's promise to His people. Their visible service will be rewarded with an immediate, visible worldly reward, as clearly stated in the Torah portion of *Bechukosai (Vayikra, chap. 26)*, and He promises swift, visible worldly punishment for visible, manifest transgressions.

He did this because the people at large can judge only things they can see, not things that are hidden. For it says, *"The hidden [sins] are for Hashem, our God, but the revealed [sins] are for us and our children forever" (Devarim 29:28)*, and *"But if the people of the land avert their eyes from that person . . . then I will direct My anger against that person" (Vayikra 20:4,5)*, [meaning, if the people ignore his open transgression, God will punish him openly.]

However, acts of service to God and sins that are hidden inside a person's heart are repaid by the Creator in this world and the World to Come. [And since these acts are concealed,] the Torah does not spell out their reward in the World to Come.

Another reason [why the Torah does not speak of the World to Come] when mentioning reward and punishment in the Torah, is because the prophet [Moshe] was addressing the Jewish people in the corporeal world of the here and now; thus he referred to tangible reward in the material world. By contrast, Yehoshua ben Yehotzadak [the Kohen Gadol] dwelt in the realm of the angels [as it says, *"Then He showed me, Yehoshua, the Kohen Gadol, standing before the angel of Hashem" (Zechariah 3:1)*]. That is why one of the angels said to him, *"I will let you walk among [the angels] who stand there" (Zechariah 3:7)*. The proper way to inspire people with hope or fear is to adapt [your promise or threat] to the time and the place [and to the level of comprehension of the audience—tangible rewards to match the earthly level of B'nei Yisrael; spiritual rewards for the angelic Yehoshua]. Understand this well.[9]

Furthermore the nature of reward in the World to Come consists of attachment to God and drawing closer to His glorious light, as it says, *"Your righteous deed will precede you, and the glory of Hashem will gather you in"* *(Yeshayah 58:8)*, *"The wise will shine like the radiance of the firmament"* *(Daniel 12:3)*, and *"To bask in the light of the living"* *(Iyov 33:30)*. Only a person who finds favor in the eyes of God can attain this nearness, and God's favor is the basis of all reward, as it says, *"For His anger endures but a moment; life results from His favor"* *(Tehillim 30:6)*. In the Torah portion of *Bechukosai* there are allusions to receiving God's favor when doing good deeds as it says, *"My Spirit will not reject you"* *(Vayikra 26:11)*, and *"I will turn My attention to you"* *(ibid. v. 9)*, and *"I will be God to you, and you will be a people to Me"* *(ibid. v. 12)*. [Looking at it this way the reward of the World to Come is indeed mentioned in the Torah].

GOD'S REWARD IS A GIFT OF GRACE

Trusting that God will reward the righteous in this world and the next, and that he will punish those who deserve to be punished is required of any believer, as it says, *"[Avram] trusted in Hashem, and He counted it as righteousness"* *(Bereishis 15:6)*, and *"Had I not trusted that I would see the goodness of Hashem in the land of life"* *(Tehillim 27:13)*. Our sages taught that the "land of life" is the World to Come (Berachos 4a).

You should not expect that as payment for your good deeds you will merit reward in this world and the World to Come. Instead, demonstrate your gratitude to the Creator for all He has done for you. Do not do good hoping for a reward in the future. After doing your best to pay your debt of gratitude to Him for the many favors He has bestowed on you, trust in God's kindness that he will

---

9. This phrase is used to indicate that the subject is dealt with extensively in Kabbalistic literature.

reward those that serve Him. As our Sages put it, "Don't be like servants who serve their master in order to receive a reward; instead be like servants who serve their master without thinking of receiving a reward. And let the awe of Heaven be upon you" (Avos 1:3); as one of the pious used to say, "No one would earn the reward of the World to Come if a strict account were taken of what a person owes God for the favors He has done for him. Reward is given only as an [undeserved] grace. Therefore, don't base your trust on reward for good deeds." And as David said, *"Yours, O Lord, is kindness, for you repay each man according to his deeds" (Tehillim 62:13).*

VII. The Reward for the Pious

The last [of the seven areas] in which one should trust in God, is trusting in the abundant outpouring of goodness God bestows on His chosen and treasured ones in the World to Come. The way to trust God is only after immersing yourself in the way of life of the pious who are worthy of this divine grace. One should live the life of the ascetic who abhors this world and exchanges its loves and desires for love of the Creator. He surrenders himself completely to God, delights only in Him, secludes himself from the world and society, and adopts the ways of prophets and holy men. [When you have done all that,] you should have faith in God that He will be gracious to you in the World to Come as He is to all holy men.

But a person who trusts that God will grant him this bliss without deserving it, is a fool and a simpleton. He is called one who "acts like Zimri [who was killed by Pinchas because of his involvement in sin with the daughters of Moav], but wants the reward of Pinchas [who zealously killed him]"(Sotah 22b).

The signs of a person on this high spiritual level are that he teaches God's servants how to serve Him, and he remains serene in the face of trial and tribulation. When it comes to fulfilling a mitzvah, nothing gets in his way, as seen from the story of the *Akeidah,* [were Avraham was willing to sacrifice his son Yitzchok to fulfill God's command], which begins, *"And God tested Avraham"*

(Bereishis 22:1), from the story of Chananiah, Mishael and Azariah who allowed themselves to be thrown into the fiery furnace [rather than worship an idol] (Daniel 3:13), from the story of Daniel in the lion's den (Daniel 6:13), and from the account of the Ten Martyrs.

If a person, [when given the choice of conversion or death,] chooses to die in the service of God rather than rebel against Him, or chooses to be poor in the service of God rather than to be rich, or chooses to be sick [and serve God] rather than be healthy [and disobey], or chooses to suffer tribulation [serving God], rather than enjoy a life of ease [and disobey], and is willing to submit to God's judgment and accept His decrees, then he deserves God's gift of delight in the World to Come. The verse has this person in mind when it says, *"I endow those who love Me with substance; I will fill their storehouses' (Mishlei 8:21)*, *"No eye has seen, God, except for You, what has been prepared for those who trust in Him" (Yeshayah 64:3)*, and *"How abundant is Your goodness that You have stored away for those who fear You" (Tehillim 31:20)*.

CHAPTER FIVE

TRUSTING IN GOD WHEN EARNING A LIVING

―――◈―――

SEVEN DIFFERENCES

When it comes to earning a living, a person who trusts in God acts differently in seven ways than one who does not.

THE FIRST: He accepts God's judgment in all things and thanks Him for both the good and the bad, as it says, *"Of kindness and justice do I sing" (Tehillim 101:1)*. Our Sages interpret this to mean, "Whether it is 'kindness' or 'justice' I will sing" (Berachos 60b). They also said, "A person should say a *berachah* for the bad, just as he says a *berachah* for the good" (Berachos 54a).

But a person who does not have faith in God brags about his prowess when things go well for him, as it says, *"The wicked man crows about his unbridled lust, and the robber praises himself that he has blasphemed God" (Tehillim 10:3)*, and he becomes angry [at God] when things go badly, as it says, *"When he will be hungry he will be angry and curse his king and his God, and direct his face upward" (Yeshayah 8:21)*.

THE SECOND: A person who trusts in God is serene, and his disposition is calm, no matter what trouble may befall him. He knows that everything is for his own good in this world and the hereafter, as David said, *"For God alone, wait silently, my soul, because my hope is from Him (Tehillim 62:6).*

But a person who does not trust in God is always troubled, forever worried, beset with sorrow and sadness, no matter whether he fares well or not. When things go well, he is unhappy because he wants more, and constantly aspires to pile up possessions. When things go badly, he is upset because his ambitions are unfulfilled, and he worries that everything will go downhill. The wise Shlomoh had such a person in mind when he said, *"All the days of a poor man are bad, but a good-hearted person feasts perpetually"* (Mishlei 15:15).

THE THIRD: A person who trusts in God does not trust his occupation to earn his living. He doesn't expect a profit or a loss from it unless God wills it. He chooses to work at his profession to obey God Who commanded us to engage in worldly pursuits in order to develop the world and provide for its needs. If through his work, he makes a profit or prevents a loss, he thanks God for it. He does not become more enamored with his profession or more devoted to it. On the contrary, his faith in God grows stronger, and he relies on Him rather than on his occupation. When he is unsuccessful, he knows that his livelihood can come from any source as long as God wishes it. He does not become disgusted with his occupation because of his failure, or give it up. Rather he continues in the service of the Creator.

But a person who does not trust in God puts his confidence in his occupation to gain profit or avoid loss. If his occupation is profitable, he praises it. He also boasts of his achievements and of his sagacity in choosing this particular occupation. He will not try anything else. If however it does not bring him profit, he gives it up, turns up his nose at it and does not want any part of it, as it says, *"Therefore, he sacrifices to his net and burns incense to his trawl"*[10] (Chavakuk 1:16).

---

10. He sacrifices to his own strength and ingenuity, which he credits with granting him the means ("nets") of his success, rather than attributing his success to God (Redak).

THE FOURTH: When a person who trusts in God has more than he needs, he spends it generously and happily on something that pleases the Creator, as it says, *"For everything is from You, and from Your hand have we given to You"* (I Divrei Hayamim 29:14).

But a person who does not trust in God thinks that he never has enough worldly possessions to satisfy his needs. He therefore saves his money, rather than spending it on fulfilling his obligations to the Creator and his fellowmen. Before he knows it, he loses his money and becomes penniless, as the wise Shlomoh said, *"One man gives generously and ends with more; another stints on doing the right thing and incurs a loss"* (Mishlei 11:24).

THE FIFTH: A person who trusts in God only involves himself in worldly affairs in order to stockpile [good deeds] for his afterlife and to make preparations for his dwelling place [in the World to Come]. He will choose an occupation which will not interfere with his Torah studies and his [Jewish] life. He will not choose a profession that would in any way undermine his Torah observance or lead him to rebel against the Creator. He does not want to become [spiritually] sick through his livelihood which was intended for his benefit.

But a person who does not trust in God places his faith in his occupation and relies on it. He will seize any opportunity that comes his way, regardless of whether it is an honest or an improper deal, without giving thought to the final outcome. As the wise Shlomoh said, *"A wise man fears and turns away from evil"* (Mishlei 14:16).

THE SIXTH: A person who trusts in God is beloved by everyone. He makes people feel at ease, because they trust he will not harm them. They have confidence in him and are not afraid that he will take their wives or their money. And he knows that no one in the world can help or hurt him. Consequently, he is not afraid of them and does not expect to benefit from them. He trusts them, and they trust him. As a result, he loves them, and they love him, as it says, *"He that trusts in Hashem, kindness surrounds him"* (Tehillim 32:10).

But a person who does not trust in God has no friends, because he is always covetous and envious of others. He imagines that any good they enjoy should be his, and that their livelihood encroaches on his livelihood. If he cannot satisfy his desires, he blames it on others, thinking that they could fulfill his needs [but refuse to do so].

If misfortune strikes, or if he loses money or a child, he believes that this was caused because others cast an evil eye on him, and that they have the ability to undo the harm and reverse his bad fortune [but do not do so]. Because of such imaginings he comes to despise people and to talk against them, to curse and to hate them. But it is he who is despised in both worlds and spurned in both dwelling places, [i.e. in both worlds], as it says, *"The perverse of heart will not find good" (Mishlei 17:20).*

The Seventh: A person who trusts God, does not grieve if he does not acquire that which he requests, or if he loses something dear to his heart. He does not hoard things that are readily available; because he is not concerned with more than today's food. He does not worry about what will happen tomorrow, because he does not know when he will meet his end. He trusts that God will grant him long life and provide him with enough food and other needs all his days. He does not rejoice in [rosy forecasts about] the future nor grieve over [ominous predictions], as it says *"Do not boast about tomorrow, for you never know what the day may bring" (Mishlei 27:1),* and as Ben Sira said, *"Do not fret about tomorrow's trouble, for you never know what the day may bring. Perhaps tomorrow you will not be here any more, and you will find yourself feeling miserable over a world that is not even your own" (Sanhedrin 100b).*

He worries and grieves about his shortcomings in serving the Creator. He does his utmost to make amends through his outward actions and inner thoughts, because he is mindful of his death and the day of his passing. Because he is afraid that he may die suddenly, he ardently prepares for his afterlife and does not care about his worldly needs. Our Sages had this in mind when they said, "Repent one day before your death" (Avos 2:15). They explained this to mean (Shabbos 153A) that a person should repent today, for he may die tomorrow. If you do that, you repent your whole life, as it says, *"Let your garments always be white" (Koheles 9:8),* [meaning, you should always be in a state of spiritual preparedness].

But a person who does not trust in God laments and complains when he is hit by a chain of misfortune, or if he loses something precious to him, or if he does not have something he wants. He stockpiles goods as if he were never going to leave this world, and puts the fear of death out of his mind as if he were immortal. Instead of concerning himself with his ultimate destiny he is busy with worldly concerns. He does not pay attention to Torah study nor does he prepare for life in the hereafter. He is convinced that he will live to a ripe old age. This stirs his worldly desires and makes him indifferent to his destiny. Should someone admonish him or advise him saying, "How long will you put off thinking about making provisions for life in the hereafter?" he answers, "I will wait until I have enough income to satisfy my needs and the needs of my wife and children for life. [When I have achieved this], and my mind is at ease, then I will take care of my obligations to the Creator, and think about making preparations for the appointed day."

CHAPTER SIX

THE SECURITY MENTALITY

———— ◆ ————

SEVEN ARGUMENTS

I think it is important to expose the foolish and false outlook [of people who want to amass enough money to last them for a lifetime, and only then think about their obligations toward God]. I call this the "security mentality" and will demonstrate in seven ways how greatly mistaken this philosophy is, even if it becomes a long-drawn-out discourse. [It is important that I do this] because it puts to shame and admonishes those who have this outlook on life. They are like the secured credit merchant, one who sells merchandise on credit to people he does not trust and demands a pledge for fear that the buyer cannot pay for the goods he bought. [Similarly, a person with this mentality does not trust God, and only after God has given him, as security, a lifetime of sustenance, is he willing to meet his obligations to Him.]

We must preface by saying: "One who thinks this way obviously doubts that the Creator rules the destiny [of man], and does not believe in His greatness. The light of his mind has been dimmed, and the lamp of his intellect has been obscured by the darkness of the sensual cravings that overpower him."

THE FIRST ARGUMENT

It is fitting to demand a security from someone who is your equal, who has no control over you, and whom you are not required to obey. But an employee would not ask his employer for a security for his salary before he started working, and certainly a slave would not ask his master for a security before doing his work. Surely, being one of God's creations, you should not demand a security from your Creator before you served Him.

How could such a thought enter one's mind. After all, for a servant to serve his master only for pay is deplorable, as the Sages said, "Do not be like servants who serve their master for the sake of receiving a reward; instead, be like servants who serve their master not for the sake of receiving a reward" (Avos 1:3). Imagine what an outrage it would be for a servant to demand a security for his salary before starting to work! As it says, *"Is this the way you repay God, you ungrateful, unwise nation?" (Devarim 32:6).*

THE SECOND ARGUMENT

The second argument is: When you take a pledge [as a security, the amount of the loan is known], therefore the security will be for a limited period. But there is no limit to the demands a person with the "security mentality" will make, because he can not possibly know how much he and his family will need in the way of food and luxuries for the rest of their lives. Even if he has much more than he needs, he will still not be content because he does not know the life expectancy of the members of his family. Because he cannot assess the time limit or the measure of his needs, he never will know how much "security" he will need.

THE THIRD ARGUMENT

The third argument is: You only demand a security from someone whom you do not owe anything and who has no just claim against you. But if you owe him money or know that he has legitimate claims against you, you will not demand a pledge from him or even accept one if he offers it.

Surely this applies to one's relationship with the Creator. We owe Him so much. Even were all the good deeds of mankind, from the time of Creation, combined in one person, they could not repay one kindness of the Creator. So how dare this shameless fellow [with the "security mentality"] demand from the Creator that He grant him additional great favors on top of the previous ones? This would only put him deeper in debt to God. Besides, he may never fulfill his vow to serve Him, because his end may be imminent.

A pious man once asked, "Folks, Do you imagine the Creator would ask you to pay Him now for debts you will incur to him tomorrow, next year or two years from now?"

"Of course not," they replied. "How can He ask us to pay now for debts that are due at a time when we may not even be alive! We only become responsible for a service when that time arrives."

Said the pious man, "By the same token, the Creator has allotted to you a specific amount of sustenance for a specific period of time. In return, you are to perform for him during that allotted time the service he demands of you. Just as He does not ask you to perform the service before its time, so too you should feel ashamed to ask Him for sustenance before the time [you need it]. Why then, do I see you asking Him for sustenance for years ahead, when you don't even know if you will live that long?" The pious man continued. "And why do you ask him to provide a livelihood for your wife, and children even before they are born? And you are not satisfied with food alone, but ask for luxuries for an indefinite time in the future. You cannot even be sure that you will be alive then. You should be giving thought not only how you neglected serving Him in the past while he was providing you with sustenance, but you should even be serving Him now in acknowledgement of all the favors He will grant in the future.

THE FOURTH ARGUMENT

The fourth argument is: When you take a security from someone, you do so for one of three reasons: (1) he might become poor and be unable to repay you; (2) he may refuse to repay, leaving you with an uncollectible debt; or (3) you are afraid he will die or disappear. Taking a security is the remedy for these defects in human relations. If you were guaranteed that none of these things would happen, it would be disgraceful to ask for a pledge.

Since none of these reasons apply to the Creator, taking a pledge from Him is utterly shameful and outrageous. As the verse says, *"Silver is Mine, and gold is Mine"* (*Chagai 2:8*), and *"Wealth and honor come from You"* (*1 Divrei Hayamim 29:12*), [thus He has the means to provide for you; so you don't need a pledge].

THE FIFTH ARGUMENT

The fifth argument is: When you take a pledge, your mind is at ease because you can either keep it for your use or profit by selling it. But you are mistaken in thinking that having your sustenance in advance would provide you with a sense of security. You can never be sure of holding on to your money; You may run into trouble and lose it, as it says, *"In the middle of his days [his wealth] will leave him"* (*Yirmeyah 17:11*).

[And, assuming that you do hold on to your money,] the argument that wealth can make you happy is false and foolish. On the contrary, wealth can be a source of worry and nervous tension, as our Sages said, "The more possessions, the more worry" (Avos 2:7).

THE SIXTH ARGUMENT

The sixth argument is: Suppose you took a pledge from someone. Had you been sure that [the lender] would pay you back before the due date, and out of the goodness of his heart, pay twice the amount he owed, in appreciation for the loan, you would not have taken a pledge from him.

We all know how kind the Creator is to us; how generous He has been and will continue to be to us; how He rewards us [in the World to Come] for our charitable deeds and service [to Him] in ways that are unfathomable and beyond description, as it says, *"No eye has seen, O God, but You, what is prepared for those that are longing for Him"* (*Yeshayah 64:3*). Just think how utterly contemptible it would be to request a pledge from Him!

THE SEVENTH ARGUMENT

The seventh argument is: One's service of Hashem is not fully his. He must count on the help of Hashem to perform His commandments. Therefore he can never consider his actions deserving of payment. You only take a pledge from someone if you are able to deliver the things for which the pledge acts as a security. But if you take a security from the Creator by asking for wealth before serving Him, you cannot live up to [your part of the bargain] of serving Him. You cannot be sure that you will be able to repay your old debts, let alone new ones. For even a righteous man can only repay God for His favors with God's own help.[11] As a devout man once said in his praises to God, "An intelligent person who knows You, will not boast about his achievements, but will attribute them to Your name and Your compassion. Because it was You who opened his heart to know You. For through Your help all offspring of Yaakov will be righteous and praise your glory, as it says, *"In God we glory at all times, and praise Your name unceasingly, Selah"* (*Tehillim 44:9*).

---

11. He can only install a *mezuzah* if God helped him to obtain a house; he can only attach *tzitzis* if God helped him to obtain a garment. The same goes for all the mitzvos.

CHAPTER SEVEN

FACTORS THAT PREVENT ONE FROM TRUSTING IN GOD

———————

Now that I have dealt with all the aspects of this topic as I see it, the time has come to discuss the things that stand in the way of trusting in God.

To begin with, everything that we mentioned in the preceding Gates that prevent you from acquiring those qualities[12] will also prevent you from trusting in God.

Another factor [that prevents you from trusting in God] is ignorance of the Creator's ways and His benevolent attributes. A person who does not appreciate how merciful the Creator is toward His creatures, how He guides them, watches over them, controls them, and how dependent they are on Him, will not have confidence in G-d, nor will he rely on Him.

Another factor [that leads to lack of trust in God] is the absence of Torah study and of studying God's commandments which warn us to rely on Him and to have faith in Him, as it says, *"Test Me, if you will, with this" (Malachi 3:10)*, and *"Trust in Hashem forever" (Yeshayah 26:4)*.

Another [factor] is the tendency to believe that the immediate, apparent cause of things [is the real cause. In other words, to think

———————

12. Believing in God's Oneness, reflecting on His Goodness, and making the commitment to serve Him.

that your profession and your skill are the sources of your wealth], without realizing that the closer a cause is to the effect, the less influence it has and the farther removed the cause is from the effect, the greater is the influence it can exert.

For example, the king who wants to punish a servant, orders his prime minister to take care of it. The prime minister orders the deputy minister, who in turn orders the chief of police, who then orders a captain, who orders a policeman, and finally the policeman carries out the order with the suitable instruments of punishment, [a whip, strap, lash or stick].

From this example we can see that the instruments of punishment themselves, [which are the immediate cause of his suffering], are the least capable of relieving or magnifying the servant's suffering, because they have no will of their own. We note that the policeman has more power than the instruments, the captain more than the policeman, the chief of police more than the captain, the deputy minister more than the chief of police, the prime minister more than the deputy minister, and the king has more power than any of them. In fact, he can pardon the servant if he wants to.

The ability of a cause to help or harm someone depends on how close or far away the cause is from the person affected. Since the Creator is the ultimate cause of all things, it is logical to trust in Him and rely on Him because of His great power to help or harm, as we explained earlier.

The gist of the concept of trust in God comes down to this: The more you know God, and the more you believe that He protects you and cares for your well being, the more you will trust in Him.

THE TEN LEVELS OF TRUST

A new-born baby trusts his mother's breasts, as it says, *"You made me trust my mother's breasts" (Tehillim 22:10)*. When his perception grows keener, he notices how much loving care his mother lavishes on him, and begins to place his trust in her, as it says, *"I swear that I stilled and silenced my soul, like a suckling child at his mother's side, like the suckling child is my soul" (Tehillim 131:2).*

As he understands even more, he sees that his mother herself looks to his father for guidance. He then begins to trust his father because of the security he provides.

When he becomes stronger and feels that he is ready to earn a living on his own—as a craftsman, merchant, or the like—he begins to trust in his own skill and ingenuity. [The reason that he trusts in his own abilities rather than in God] is because he is unaware of all the kindness God has bestowed on him until now.

To illustrate this, one of the pious men used to tell a story about his neighbor, a talented scribe, who earned his living working at his craft.

"How are you doing?" the pious man asked the scribe.

"As long as my hand is in good shape, I'm fine," the scribe replied.

That night, the scribe's hand was cut off so that for the rest of his life he was unable to write. This was his divine punishment for trusting in his hand [instead of relying on God].

If the man [is not self employed, rather he] earns a living working for someone else, he shifts his trust to his employer and begins to depend on him.

When he understands further and sees how every person has deficiencies, and everyone needs help from the Creator, he begins to trust in God. He relies on Him for things over which he has no control and about which he has no option other than to submit to the Creator's decree, such as the rainfall in the planting season, acquiring water when sailing the seas or crossing barren deserts, during flash floods, when an epidemic strikes, and all kinds of situations where man is completely powerless, as it says, *"In their time of distress they will say, 'Arise and save us!'" (Yirmeyah 2:27).*

When his recognition of God becomes clearer, He begins to trust in God even in matters over which he has some control. If he was earning a living through a dangerous or exhausting profession, he will quit this job, trusting in God that He will provide him with an easier way to earn a living. [Yet he will believe that ultimately his livelihood came on account of his efforts.]

As his understanding of God increases further, he begins to trust that after all his efforts—both the difficult and the easy ones—it is God who is providing for his needs. He pursues his occupation only because it is God's command that man must actively pursue a livelihood.

When he gains a deeper understanding of God's compassion on His creatures, he will accept God's decrees wholeheartedly, outwardly and inwardly. He will be happy with whatever God brings upon him, whether death or life, poverty or wealth, health or illness. He only longs for what God chooses for him. He only desires what God wants him to have. He submits to God, and surrenders his body and soul to His judgment. In worldly matters he will not favor one thing over another, or wish he were in a different situation than the present one. As one who trusted God said, "I never arose in the morning in one place and wished I were someplace else."

When his recognition of God becomes clearer yet, he begins to understand why he was created and placed in this transitory world. He grasps the loftiness of the next world, which is the permanent one, and will have no stomach for this world and its lusts. He will retreat [from society] to be alone with God in thought, soul, and body. He will delight in remembering Him in solitude and banish from his mind all thoughts other than the greatness of God. When he finds himself in a large gathering [he will not socialize]. He wants only to please God and yearns to draw himself nearer to Him. The joy he derives from his love of God is greater than the gratification others derive from worldly pleasures. It is even greater than the delight the soul experiences in the World to Come. This is the highest level of trust in God, a stage that was attained by the prophets, the pious, and the pure who are God's treasure. For it says, *"Even on the path of Your judgments, Hashem, we put our hopes in You; Your name and Your mention, the yearning of our soul"* (*Yeshayah 26:8*), and *"My soul thirsts for God, the living God"* (*Tehillim 42:3*).

These are the ten levels of trust. A person who trusts is certain to be on one of these levels.

In conclusion, it is interesting to note that there are ten synonyms for the word "trust" in Hebrew, each of which matches one of these ten levels. There is *mivtach*—trust, *mish'an*—support, *tikvah*—hope, *machaseh*—refuge, *tocheles*—anticipation, *chikui*—awaiting, *semichah*—dependence, *sever*—expectation, *mis'ad*—help, and *kesel*—confidence.

May God in His mercy place us among those who trust in Him and surrender themselves outwardly and inwardly to His judgment. Amen.

This completes the Gate of Trust,
for God, the last and the first.

GLOSSARY

———— ◈ ————

AKEIDAH – when Isaac was bound on the altar for a sacrifice
AVRAHAM – Abraham

B'NEI YISRAEL – Children of Israel
BAMIDBAR – The Book of Numbers
BEIS MIDRASH – study hall
BERACHAH pl. *BERACHOS*: – blessing
BEREISHIS – The Book of Genesis
BITACHON – trust

CHAGAI – Haggai
CHAVAKUK – Habakuk

DAVEN – pray
DEVARIM – The Book of Deuteronomy
DIVREI HAYAMIM – The Book of Chronicles

EICHA – The Book of Lamentations
ELIYAHU – Elijah
ERETZ YISRAEL – The Land of Israel

HALACHAH – law
HASHEM – God
HASHEM YISBARACH – God may He be blessed
HOSHEA – The Book of Hosea

IYOV – Job

KARES – punishment of premature death
KAVANAH – intent
KOHELES – Ecclesiastes
KOHEN GADOL – High Priest

LULAV – palm branch take on Sukkos

MATZAH – unleavened bread
MELACHIM – The Book of Kings
MEZUZAH – parchment scroll containing the Shema that is placed on the doorpost.
MISHLEI – Proverbs
MISHNAH – compilation of the oral tradition; it also refers to one paragraph of this compilation
MITZVAH pl. *MITZVOS*: – commandment
MOAV – Moab
MOSHE – Moses

NACHUM – Nahum

OVADYAH – Obadiah

PINCHAS – Phineas

SEFER – book
SHAAR HABITACHON – The Gate of Trust
SHABBOS – Saturday the day of rest
SHEMOS – The Book of Exodus
SHLOMOH – Solomon
SHLOMOH HAMELECH – King Solomon
SHMUEL – The Book of Samuel
SHOFAR – Ram's horn blown on Rosh Hashana
SHOFTIM – The Book of Judges
SIDRAH – portion of the Torah

SUKKAH – hut used on Sukkos
SUKKOS – Festival of Tabernacles

TEFILLIN – phylacteries
TEHILLIM – Psalms
TESHUVA – Repentance
TZEFANIAH – Zephaniah
TZITZIS – fringes worn on a four cornered garment

VAYIKRA – The Book of Leviticus

YAAKOV – Jacob
YECHEZKEL – Ezekiel
YEHOSHUA – Joshua
YESHAYAH – Isaiah
YESHIVAH – academy
YETZER HARA – evil inclination
YIRMIYAH – Jeremiah
YISHAI – Jesse
YISRAEL – Israel
YITZCHOK – Isaac
YONAH – Jonah